A Companion of
Prayer
for
Daily Living

A Companion of Prayer for Daily Living

PREPARED AND EDITED BY
MASSEY H. SHEPHERD, JR.

MOREHOUSE-BARLOW CO., INC.
WILTON, CONNECTICUT

ISBN No. 0-8192-1230-X
Library of Congress Catalog Card Number: 78-62062

© 1978 by Morehouse-Barlow Co., Inc.
78 Danbury Road, Wilton, Connecticut 06897

Printed in the United States of America

Foreword

THE treasures of Christian prayer and praise are a heritage that is immeasurable. They have come to us from all ages of the Church's life and witness, and from the hearts and hands of so many devoted men and women, known and unknown. This manual is but a small collection from sources old and new. Only a few that are familiar in our liturgies and hymns have been included, because they are more accessible to us; and some of these have been given either in their original form or in a new translation. I have also been bold to offer, at the publishers' request, some prayers and devotions of my own.

In all anthologies of prayers an editor alters and adapts, lengthens or shortens forms according to the needs of those whom he hopes will use and pray them. This book is no exception. In such cases I have added an asterisk (*) to prayers that I have changed; but I have tried not to alter their basic substance and intent.

It is often difficult to determine the original source and wording of prayers that have come into common use in the many manuals of this kind. If I have failed to discover them, or if I have violated any copyright, I shall be glad to amend my fault. To those publishers who have graciously given me permission to use their copyrighted material, I offer my sincere thanks. A list of them is included at the end of this book.

Massey H. Shepherd, Jr.

Pentecost, 1978

Contents

Introduction

PRAYER is the lifting up of our minds and hearts to God. A life of prayer is a life in God. If we truly believe in God and trust him, we know that he is always near us and that he wills for us only what is good. Nothing can ever separate us from his love for us. We do not always have to be consciously listening or talking to him. Prayer is more than words. It may be times of awareness of God in silence. Often it is an inner serenity of spirit in the midst of affairs and of busy activities, because we have committed our lives in trust to him.

God wants us to call upon him, whatever may be our problems, our needs, or our circumstances. He is always ready to listen to us and to accept us as we are in any situation. We should never be afraid or anxious about addressing him. If we think we are unworthy of his attention, we are wrong. He knows and loves us better than we know or love ourselves. He loves each one of us as though each were his only child, his only friend. He made us and we belong to him. He will never lose sight of us nor will he abandon us for any reason.

We all experience times of stress or of sorrow when we may doubt God's love. He knows this and we need not be ashamed. When we do have doubts or fears, we should tell him about them frankly. If we do not, we shut our-

1

selves off from him when we need him most. He knows our needs before we ask and our ignorance in asking. If we do not ask, we shall not find; if we do not knock, the door will not be opened. It is by praying that we learn from him how to pray, for he teaches us.

What God does expect from us is that we be sincere and honest with him in our prayers. We cannot deceive him; much less can we manipulate him. This is not the way of love. Only by being open to him can our love grow. Real love can bear anything and everything, because love is patient and full of hope. Love receives because it gives; and the more it gives, the more it receives. This is the miracle of love.

Our Lord Jesus Christ taught us how to pray and gave us his example. He taught us that God hears and answers every prayer offered in sincerity and truth, and that God gives us more than we desire or deserve. By his example, he showed us that prayer is acceptance of God's will for us and our obedience to him, for which he gives his grace and help. Christian prayer, therefore, is always in the Name and for the sake of our Lord Jesus. It is letting his prayer work in and through us; for he continually intercedes for us in heaven before his Father and ours. True prayer is not bringing God's will to conform to ours, but in lifting our wills to conform to his. Only in his will do we find our peace.

Each one of us must find his or her pattern and rhythm of daily prayer. It takes time and effort. Regular times set apart for our prayers help us to gain the habit of it, and growth and effectiveness in it; but they need not be prolonged. Nor is there any special style of praying, other than that it be sincere and natural to us. We may prefer it to be formal and conventional, or we may speak as simply and familiarly as we do to our best friend. There can be no irreverence where no irreverence is intended. Our hearts always pray better than our lips can ever speak.

We should never neglect participation in corporate prayer with others of Christian faith, for they need our support in prayer as we need theirs. The Church's liturgy informs our personal prayer and preserves it from being self-centered and eccentric. In the liturgy we learn our priorities of prayer: the great things — God's kingdom and his righteousness — so that the little things may be added. From the liturgy we also learn how to broaden and deepen the attitudes and concerns of prayer, and to enter sympathetically into the full range of prayer in the communion of saints of all ages and places. On the other hand, our personal life of prayer should help us to make the corporate prayer of the Church come alive to us, and save us from experiencing it as a routine formality.

Christian prayer is always offered in the context of adoration and thanksgiving. If we first count our blessings in acknowledgment of whence they come, we shall be more ready to confess our sins and shortcomings and to ask what is appropriate for ourselves and for others. We shall know God more perfectly by praising him than by petitioning him. The praise of God is in itself its own reward: "to know him more clearly, love him more dearly, and follow him more nearly."

— M. H. S.

I. Prayer at All Times and in All Places

THE LORD'S PRAYER

1   OUR Father in heaven,
    hallowed be your Name,
    your kingdom come,
    your will be done,
      on earth as in heaven.
Give us today our daily bread.
Forgive us our sins
    as we forgive those who sin against us.
Save us from the time of trial,
    and deliver us from evil.
For the kingdom, the power, and the glory are yours
    now and for ever. Amen.

— Saint Matthew 6:9-13

[Translation of the International Consultation on
English Texts, in *Prayers We Have in Common* 1975]

FOR THE SPIRIT OF PRAYER

2   YOU are great, O Lord, and worthy of highest praise. You stir in us the joy of praising you, since you have made us for yourself, and our hearts are restless until they rest in you.

Grant me, Lord, to know and understand what comes first: whether to call on you or to praise you, or to know you before I call on you. But who can call on you without knowing you? For if I do not know you, I might call on someone other than you. Or, is it that I should call on you so that I may know you? But 'how shall they call on him in whom they have not believed; or how shall they believe without a preacher'? But 'they who seek the Lord shall find him.' For they 'who seek him shall find him,' and finding him shall praise him.

—Saint Augustine

5

3   O ALMIGHTY God, from whom every good prayer cometh, and who pourest out on all who desire it the Spirit of grace and supplications: Deliver us, when we draw nigh to thee, from coldness of heart and wanderings of mind; that with steadfast thoughts and kindled affections we may worship thee in spirit and in truth; through Jesus Christ our Lord. Amen.

— William Bright

4   O GOD of peace, who hast taught us that in returning and in rest we shall be saved, in quietness and in confidence shall be our strength: By the might of thy Spirit lift us, we pray thee, to thy presence, where we may be still and know that thou art God; through Jesus Christ our Lord. Amen.

— John W. Suter, Jr.

5   UNCROWD our hearts, O God, until silence speaks in thy still small voice; turn us from the hearing of words, and the making of words, and the confusion of much speaking, that we may possess ourselves in these brief moments undistracted, waiting, with all our hopes listening for thy footfall. Amen.

— Samuel H. Miller

FOR MEDITATION ON THE SCRIPTURES

6   BLESSED Lord, who hast caused all holy Scriptures to be written for our learning: Grant that we may in such wise hear them, read, mark, learn, and inwardly digest them; that we may embrace and ever hold fast the blessed hope of everlasting life, which thou hast given us in our Saviour Jesus Christ. Amen.

—Thomas Cranmer*

7   O LORD Jesus Christ, who art the truth incarnate
and the teacher of the faithful: Let thy Spirit over-
shadow us in reading thy Word, and conform our
thoughts to thy revelation; that learning of thee
with honest hearts, we may be rooted and built up
in thee, who livest and reignest with the Father and
the Holy Spirit, one God, now and ever. Amen.

— *William Bright*

8   O GOD, in ages past you inspired holy men and
women to set forth your truth in song and story,
in prophecy and precept: Illumine our minds and
attune our hearts to hear and understand what you
have revealed through them in your holy Word;
that we may apply their lessons in our lives and
to our times; through Jesus Christ our Lord. Amen.

— *M. H. S.*

9   LET not thy Word, O Lord, become a judgment upon
us, that we hear it and do it not, that we know it
and love it not, that we believe it and obey it not,
O thou, who with the Father and the Holy Spirit
livest and reignest, world without end. Amen.

— Ascribed to *Thomas a Kempis*

PRAYERS FOR ALL OCCASIONS

10   LORD Jesus Christ, Son of God,
have mercy on me, a sinner.

— *The Jesus Prayer*

11   O GOD, the light of the minds that know you, the
joy of the hearts that love you, and the strength
of the wills that serve you: Grant us so to know
you that we may truly love you, so to love you
that we may fully serve you, whom to serve is
perfect freedom; through Jesus Christ our Lord.
Amen.

— Ascribed to *Saint Augustine*

12   CHRIST be with me, Christ within me,
Christ behind me, Christ before me,
Christ beside me, Christ to win me,
Christ to comfort and restore me.

Christ beneath me, Christ above me,
Christ in quiet, Christ in danger,
Christ in hearts of all that love me,
Christ in mouth of friend and stranger.

— Saint Patrick's Breastplate
[Translated by *Cecil Frances Alexander*]

13   ALMIGHTY God, who alone gavest us the breath of life, and alone canst keep alive in us the breathing of holy desires: We beseech thee for thy compassion's sake to sanctify all our thoughts and endeavors, that we may neither begin an action without a pure intention, nor continue it without thy blessing; and grant that, having the eyes of our understanding purged to behold things invisible and unseen, we may in heart be inspired with thy wisdom, and in work be upheld by thy strength, and in the end be accepted of thee, as thy faithful servants, having done all things to thy glory, and thereby to our endless peace. Amen.

— Rowland Williams

14   GRANT, O Lord, that I may live in thy fear, die in thy favor, rest in thy peace, rise in thy power, reign in thy glory; for thy only beloved Son's sake, Jesus Christ our Lord. Amen.

— William Laud

15   TEACH us, good Lord, to serve thee as thou deservest, to give and not to count the cost, to fight and not to heed the wounds, to toil and not to seek for rest, to labor and to ask for no reward, save that of knowing that we do thy will; through Jesus Christ our Lord. Amen.

— Saint Ignatius Loyola

16   O GOD, day by day lead us deeper into the mystery of life, and make us interpreters of life to our fellows; through Jesus Christ our Lord. Amen.

— Henry Sylvester Nash

17   LORD, make me an instrument of your peace.
Where there is hatred, let us sow love;
Where there is injury, pardon;
Where there is discord, union;
Where there is doubt, faith;
Where there is despair, hope;
Where there is darkness, light;
Where there is sadness, joy.

Grant that we may not so much seek
to be consoled, as to console;
to be understood, as to understand;
to be loved, as to love.

For it is in giving that we receive;
it is in pardoning that we are pardoned;
and it is in dying that we are born to eternal life.
Amen.

— Ascribed to *Saint Francis*

18 ALMIGHTY God, Father of all mercies,
we your unworthy servants give you humble thanks
for all your goodness and loving-kindness
to us and to all whom you have made.

We bless you for our creation, preservation,
and all the blessings of this life;
but above all for your immeasurable love
in the redemption of the world by our Lord Jesus
Christ;
for the means of grace, and for the hope of glory.

And, we pray, give us such an awareness of your
mercies,
that with truly thankful hearts we may
show forth your praise,
not only with our lips, but in our lives,
by giving up our selves to your service,
and by walking before you
in holiness and righteousness all our days;
through Jesus Christ our Lord,
to whom, with you and the Holy Spirit,
be honor and glory throughout all ages. Amen.

— *Edward Reynolds* *
[Revised, *The Book of Common Prayer, Proposed*]

II. Daily Praise and Prayer

Hymns

19   NOW that the daylight fills the sky,
We lift our hearts to God on high,
That he, in all we do or say,
Would keep us free from harm today:

Would guard our hearts and tongues from strife;
From anger's din would hide our life;
From all ill sights would turn our eyes;
Would close our ears from vanities:

Would keep our inmost conscience pure;
Our souls from folly would secure;
Would bid us check the pride of sense
With due and holy abstinence.

So we, when this new day is gone,
And night in turn is drawing on,
With conscience by the world unstained
Shall praise his Name for vict'ry gained.

               — *Office Hymn for Prime*
          [Translated by *John Mason Neale*]

20   CHRIST whose glory fills the skies,
    Christ, the true, the only Light,
Sun of Righteousness, arise,
    Triumph o'er the shades of night!
Day-spring from on high, be near!
Day-star, in my heart appear!

Dark and cheerless is the morn
    Unaccompanied by thee;
Joyless is the day's return,
    Till thy mercy's beams I see;
Till they inward light impart,
Glad my eyes, and warm my heart.

Visit then this soul of mine,
    Pierce the gloom of sin and grief!

Fill me, Radiancy Divine,
  Scatter all my unbelief!
More and more thyself display,
Shining to the perfect day!

— *Charles Wesley*

Psalm

21 BLESS the LORD, O my soul;
      with all my being, bless his holy Name!
    Bless the LORD, O my soul,
      and forget not all his benefits.
    He forgives all your sins,
      and heals all your diseases.
    He redeems your life from the grave,
      and crowns you with mercy and loving-kindness.
    He fills all your years with good,
      and renews your youth like an eagle's.

    The LORD gives righteous judgments,
      and justice for all who are oppressed.
    He made known his ways to Moses,
      and his deeds to the children of Israel.
    The LORD is merciful and compassionate,
      slow to anger and rich in loving-kindness.
    He will not always scold us,
      nor will he keep his anger for ever.
    He has not treated or punished us,
      as our sins and misdeeds deserve.

    As high as the heavens are above the earth,
      so great is his mercy to those who revere him.
    As far as the east is from the west,
      so far has he removed our sins from us.
    As a father has compassion for his children,
      so the LORD has compassion for those who revere
        him.
    For he knows of what we are made;
      he remembers that we are but dust.
    The love of the LORD for those who revere him
      endures for ever and ever.

— *Psalm 103:1-14, 17*

12

22 HEAVENLY Father, in you we live and move and
have our being: We humbly pray you so to guide
and govern us by your Holy Spirit, that in all the
cares and occupations of our life we may not forget you, but may remember that we are ever walking in your sight; through Jesus Christ our Lord.
Amen.

— Anon.

23 BLESS us, O God, with the vision of thy being and
beauty, that in the strength of it we may work
without haste and without rest; through Jesus
Christ our Lord. Amen.

— Henry Sylvester Nash

24 LORD Jesus Christ, Son of the living God: Help me
this day to love and serve you in everyone I meet,
and to rejoice in your promise to be with me
always, as my Savior and my Lord. Amen.

— M. H. S.

25 O GOD, this is the first day of the rest of my life.
Fill my heart with the inward joy and serenity
that comes from living close to you; that by your
Spirit I may bear whatever ills and crosses that I
meet with a good courage and endure what I must
endure; and always and in all things give you
thanks; for the sake of my Lord Jesus Christ. Amen.

— M. H. S.

26 O LORD, thou knowest how busy I must be this day.
If I forget thee, do not thou forget me. Amen.

— Sir Jacob Astley

Confession

27 MOST merciful God, I confess that I have sinned against you in thought, word, and deed. I have not loved you with my whole heart; I have not loved my neighbors as myself. I pray you of your mercy forgive what I have been, amend what I am, and direct what I shall be; that I may delight in your will, and walk in your ways; through Jesus Christ our Lord. Amen.

*— Services for Trial Use**

Intercession

28 REMEMBER this day, O Lord, in your love:
    my family, friends, and neighbors,
        and all whom I know and love, near and far;
    all your people in their several vocations:
        my Bishop and my priest and the faithful laity;
        my employers and fellow-workers;
        and those who govern us in freedom and in peace.

Remember this day, O Lord, in your mercy
    all who are in any need or trouble,
        and those who minister to them;
    all who are lonely, tempted, or afraid,
        and the forgotten ones whom you alone know;
    Those whom I should but cannot remember,
        and those this day who are appointed to die.
Remember me also, a sinner, for Jesus' sake. Amen.

— M. H. S.

Doxology

29 GLORY to God, whose power, working in us, can do infinitely more than we can ask or imagine: Glory to him from generation to generation in the Church, and in Christ Jesus for ever and ever. Amen.

— Ephesians 3:20-21

14

Psalms

30 BLESSED be the Name of the LORD
now and for evermore.
From the rising of the sun to its setting,
let the Name of the LORD be praised.

The LORD looks down from heaven
upon all who inhabit the earth.
He molded the hearts of all of them,
and discerns all their doings.

— Psalms 113:2-3; 33:13-15

Prayers

31 BLESSED Savior, at this hour you hung upon the
Cross, stretching out your loving arms: Grant
that all the peoples of the earth may look to you
and be saved; for your mercies' sake. Amen.

— Traditional

32 ALMIGHTY and everlasting God, in Christ you have
revealed your glory among the nations: Preserve
the works of your mercy, that your Church throughout the world may persevere with steadfast faith in
the confession of your Name; through Jesus Christ
our Lord. Amen.

— Gelasian Sacramentary

33 ALMIGHTY God, our heavenly Father: Guide, we
beseech thee, the nations of the world into the
way of justice and truth, and establish among
them that peace which is the fruit of righteousness,
that they may become the Kingdom of our Lord
and Savior Jesus Christ. Amen.

— Edward Lambe Parsons

34   REMEMBER at this hour, O Lord, in your mercy
those whom I bear in my heart before you (NN.
. . .). Enfold them in the arms of your love;
guard them in all temptation and danger; and
keep their hearts and minds in your peace, now
and always, for your mercies' sake. Amen.

— M. H. S.

EVENING

Hymns

35   O JOYFUL Light, pure splendor
of the immortal, heavenly Father,
holy, blessed Jesus Christ:

As we come to the setting of the sun
and behold the evening light,
we hymn the praise of Father, Son,
and Holy Spirit divine.

You are worthy at all times
to be praised by reverent voices,
O Son of God, Giver of life;
therefore the world gives you glory.

— Greek Vesper Hymn
[Translation by *M. H. S.*]

36   THE day thou gavest, Lord, is ended,
The darkness falls at thy behest;
To thee our morning prayers ascended,
Thy praise shall sanctify our rest.

We thank thee that thy Church, unsleeping
While earth rolls onward into light
Through all the world her watch is keeping,
And rests not now by day or night.

As o'er each continent and island
    The dawn leads on another day,
The voice of prayer is never silent,
    Nor dies the strain of praise away.

The sun that bids us rest is waking
    Our brethren 'neath the western sky,
And hour by hour fresh lips are making
    Thy wondrous doings heard on high.

So be it, Lord; thy throne shall never,
    Like earth's proud empires, pass away:
Thy kingdom stands, and grows for ever,
    Till all thy creatures own thy sway.

— John Ellerton

Psalm

37 O LORD, you have searched me,
        and know me thoroughly.
    You know whether I sit down or stand up;
        you can discern my thought from afar.

    You watch where I walk and lie down,
        and are familiar with all my ways.
    There is not a word on my lips,
        but you, LORD, know it already.

    You surround me behind and before;
        your hand is ever laid upon me.
    Such knowledge is too wonderful for me,
        so high that I cannot reach it.

    Where shall I escape from your Spirit?
        Where can I flee from your presence?
    If I climb up to heaven, you are there;
        you are there, if my bed be in the underworld.

    If I take wing to the dawning sun,
        or dwell at the limits of the sea,
    Even there will your hand lead me,
        and your right hand will hold on to me.

17

If I say, "Surely the darkness will hide me,
    and the night will cover me round about" —
Yet darkness is not dark to you,
    for the night is as bright as the day;
    darkness and light to you are both alike.

— Psalm 139:1-12

Prayers

38   LIGHTEN our darkness, we beseech thee, O Lord;
and by thy great mercy defend us from all perils
and dangers of this night; for the love of thy only
Son, our Savior, Jesus Christ. Amen.

— Gelasian Sacramentary

39   O GOD, who wouldest fold both heaven and earth
in a single peace: Let the design of thy great love
lighten upon the waste of our wraths and sorrows;
and give peace to thy Church, peace among the
nations, peace in our dwellings, and peace in our
hearts; through thy Son our Savior Jesus Christ.
Amen.

— Eric Milner-White

40   O GOD, whose days are without end, and whose
mercies cannot be numbered: Make us, we beseech
thee, deeply sensible of the shortness and uncer-
tainty of human life; and let thy Holy Spirit lead
us in holiness and righteousness all our days; that,
when we shall have served thee in our generation,
we may be gathered unto our fathers, having the
testimony of a good conscience; in the communion
of the Catholic Church; in the confidence of a
certain faith; in the comfort of a reasonable, religious, and holy hope; in favor with thee our God,
and in perfect charity with the world. All which
we ask through Jesus Christ our Lord. Amen.

— Jeremy Taylor*

41   FORGIVE me, Lord, for thy dear Son,
The ill that I this day have done;
That with the world, myself, and thee,
I, ere I sleep, at peace may be.

— Thomas Ken

Intercession

42   REMEMBER this night, O Lord, in your goodness:
Those who stand guard for us while we rest;
those who work to serve our needs on the morrow;
those who comfort the suffering and the bereaved;
those who minister to and wait upon the dying.
Grant that as we know their watching, so we may
share their loving care; through Jesus Christ our
Lord. Amen.

— M. H. S.

43   O LORD of all mercy, grant thy peace through this
long night especially
to those who find no surcease from pain of body;
to those who struggle against hidden adversaries;
to those who are tangled in the terrors of the
unbalanced mind;
to those who bear a shame they cannot evade and
for which they will not repent;
to those who must meet death although the tasks
of life seem unfinished.
Grant to each according to his need, and by thy
loving-kindness manifested in the mystery of such
dark hours bring such comfort as could come only
from thee. Amen.

— Samuel H. Miller

44   TO our prayers, O Lord, we join our unfeigned thanks
for all thy mercies: for our being, our reason, and
all other endowments and faculties of soul and
body; for our health, friends, food, and raiment,
and all the other comforts and conveniences of
life.

Above all, we adore thy mercy in sending thy only
Son into the world, to redeem us from sin and
eternal death, and in giving us the knowledge and
sense of our duty towards thee.

We bless thee for thy patience with us, notwith-
standing our many and great provocations; for all
the directions, assistances, and comforts of thy
Holy Spirit; for thy continual care and watchful
providence over us through the whole course of our
lives; and particularly for the mercies and benefits
of the past day;

Beseeching thee to continue these thy blessings to
us, and to give us grace to show our thankfulness
in a sincere obedience to his laws, through whose
merits and intercession we received them all, thy
Son our Saviour Jesus Christ. Amen.

— Book of Common Prayer

Conclusion

45   MAY the souls of the faithful departed
    through the mercy of God rest in peace.
Rest eternal grant to them, O Lord;
    and let light perpetual shine upon them. Amen.

— Traditional

46   The LORD bless us and keep us.
The LORD make his face to shine upon us,
    and be gracious unto us.
The LORD lift up his countenance upon us,
    and give us peace, now and evermore. Amen.

— Numbers 6:24-26

III. Daily Life and Work

THE FAMILY

Grace at Meals

47   BLESSED art thou, O LORD God, King of the Universe, who bringest forth food from the earth, and sustainest all your creatures with goodness, grace and mercy. Blessed art thou, who givest food to all. Amen.

— *Jewish*

48   WE thank you, Lord, for these gifts of your bounty. In our plenty may we not forget the poor and needy; and for all your mercies make us humbly grateful. Amen.

— *M. H. S.*

49   BE present at our table, Lord;
BE here and everywhere adored.
These creatures bless, and grant that we
May feast in Paradise with thee. Amen.

— *John Wesley*

50   O THOU who clothest the lilies
and feedest the birds of the sky:
who leadest the lambs to the pasture
and the hart to the waterside:
who hast multiplied loaves and fishes
and converted water into wine;
do thou come to our table
as guest and giver to dine. Amen.

— *Anon.*

51   BLESSED are you, O Lord: You have fed us from our earliest days; and you give food to every living creature. Fill our hearts with joy and gladness; that, having always what is sufficient for us, we may abound the more in every good work of mercy; for the sake of Christ Jesus our Lord, through whom be to you glory, honor, and power now and for ever. Amen.

— Apostolic Constitutions

For our Home

52   HEAVENLY Father, from whom every family is named: Look with favor on our home. Defend us

from all evil and supply our needs, according to your gracious will. Give us love and joy in our companionship with one another, and with all who share in hospitality. Bless our going out and our coming in. Wherever our paths may lead, keep us near to you and one another, in prayer and in the knowledge that you enfold us in your never-failing care and love; through Jesus Christ our Lord. Amen.

— M. H. S.

For Wife or Husband

53   BLESS, O Lord, your servant N., my wife [*or*, husband], and let your gracious hand be with *her* night and day. Give *her* health of body and spirit, and support *her* in all necessities. Strengthen *her* in all temptations; comfort *her* in all sorrows; and sustain *her* in all changes. Make us both to increase in love and care for each other, and to dwell with you for ever in your favor, in the light of your countenance, and in your glory; through Jesus Christ our Lord. Amen.

*— Jeremy Taylor**

54 BLESS our children, NN., O Lord of infinite mercy,
with healthful bodies, with good understandings,
with the graces and gifts of your Spirit, with sweet
dispositions and holy habits; and sanctify them
throughout in their bodies and souls and spirits,
and keep them unblamable to the Coming of the
Lord Jesus. Amen.

— *Jeremy Taylor**

55 O GOD of love and mercy, help us to understand
our children as they grow in years and in knowledge of your world. Make us compassionate for
their temptations and failures, and encouraging
in their seeking after truth and value for their lives.
Stir in us appreciation of their ideals, and sympathy
for their frustrations; that with them we may
look for a better world than either we or they have
known, through Jesus Christ our common Lord
and Master. Amen.

— *M. H. S.*

56 ALMIGHTY God, in whose hands the great stars
and vast seasons move with quiet beauty and
sure design: We pray thee for this child, N. [*or,*
these children, NN.], in whose heart and mind the
glory of creation breaks as if for the first time, and

for whose soul the ancient adversaries are joined
in conflict as in early Eden. Lead *him* through
this maze of life and death tenderly, yet with such
strengthening benedictions that in all *his* growing
responsibilities *he* may find the joy and peace of
eternal life. Keep alive in *him* the grace of thy
Spirit, lest *he* lose the birthright of that wondrous
image with which thou didst first create *him*. Amen.

— *Samuel H. Miller*

57   O GOD, whose fatherly care reacheth to the utter-
      most parts of the earth: We humbly beseech thee
      graciously to behold and bless those whom we love,
      now absent from us. Defend them from all dangers
      of soul and body; and grant that both they and
      we, drawing nearer to thee, may be bound together
      by thy love in the communion of thy Holy Spirit,
      and in the fellowship of thy saints; through Jesus
      Christ our Lord. Amen.

                    — *Book of Common Prayer*

ANNIVERSARIES

My own Birthday

58   HEAVENLY Father, the span of my life is in your
      keeping, and you know all my thoughts and my
      ways. Draw me ever closer to you in loving obe-
      dience to your will, with a grateful heart for
      your past mercies and for your forgiveness of my
      sins and failures. Renew a right spirit within me.
      Give me new understanding and strength to serve
      you better in my daily tasks, and be more loving
      to others. Keep me firm in my trust that, whether
      in life or in death, you are my help and my defense,
      for the sake of Jesus my Lord and Savior. Amen.

                                      — *M. H. S.*

Birthday of a Loved One

59   KEEP watch, O Lord, in your loving care over my
      loved one, N, as *his* days increase. Guard and
      guide *him* wherever *he* may be. Strengthen *him*
      in faith and hope; and, if *he* fall, raise *him* up.
      Comfort *him* when discouraged or sorrowful;
      and keep *his* mind and heart serene in your peace
      all *his* days, for Jesus' sake. Amen.

                    —*Book of Common Prayer**

For Baptism

60   HEAVENLY Father, in my baptism you made me a living member of the body of your Son and sealed me with the sign of his cross, that I should never be ashamed to acknowledge him before the world. Grant me this and every day to hold in my heart the remembrance of his death for me and his life in me; that he may shield me in temptation, stir me in faith, comfort me in hope, and excite me in love, unto my life's end. Amen.

— M. H. S.

For Confirmation

61   O GOD, my heavenly Father, I thank you for confirming me with the strengthening gifts of grace of your Holy Spirit. Increase in me daily a consecration to your service as a responsible witness to the gospel of my Lord. Keep me mindful of your presence with me in all the temptations and adventures that I meet, and faithful to you always to my life's end; for the sake of Jesus Christ, my Lord and Savior. Amen.

— M. H. S.

For Marriage

62   O GOD, our Heavenly Father, we thank you for the grace and blessing you have bestowed on us in the days and years of our marriage. Let our love for each other be pure and enduring. Give us understanding of each other's minds and needs. Help us to share our joys and sorrows; and keep us ever faithful to our promise to live together according to your will; through Jesus Christ our Lord. Amen.

— Prayers for All Occasions*

63 O FATHER of all, we pray to thee for those whom
we love, but see no longer [and especially for N.].
Grant *them* thy peace; let light perpetual shine
upon *them;* and in thy loving wisdom and almighty
power work in *them* the good purpose of thy
perfect will; through Jesus Christ our Lord. Amen.

—*Book of Common Prayer*, [English Proposed, 1928]

FOR FRIENDS

64 O GOD, who hast made pleasant and lovely the
bonds of friendship: I thank thee for the many
friends and comrades with whom thou hast enriched my life [and especially for NN.]. Tighten
the cords of love which unite us in thee, and in
death divide us not; through Jesus Christ our Lord.
Amen.   — *Charles Henry Brent*

65 O ETERNAL God, who watchest over all: Grant
that the friendships formed between us here may
neither through sin be broken, nor hereafter
through life's changes be forgotten; but that bound
together in the comradeship of thy glad service,
we may be drawn nearer to thee and to each other;
through Jesus Christ our Lord. Amen.

— *A Book of Prayers for Schools*

66 WE give thee thanks, O God, for those who mean
so much to us:
Those to whom we can go at any time;
those to whom we can go when we are tired,
knowing that they have the gift of rest;
those with whom we can talk, and keep nothing
back, knowing that they will not laugh at our
dreams or mock our failures;
those in whose presence it is easier to be good;
those in whose company joys are doubly dear, and
sorrows are soothed;
those who by their warning, their counsel, and
their rebuke have kept us from mistakes we

might have made, and sins we might have committed.

Above all we thank thee for Jesus, the Lord of our hearts, and the Savior of our souls; in whose Name accept this our thanksgiving. Amen.

— *William Barclay* *

OUR DAILY WORK

67   LORD, be with me as I go to my work today. Help me to be faithful in the discharge of my duties, and honorable in all my dealings. Give me self-control in speech and temper; and let me be a good example to others of Christian humility and thoughtfulness; for the sake of Jesus Christ my Savior. Amen.   — *Prayers for All Occasions*

68   O LORD GOD, quicken in us the spirit of courage; that we may go forth with hopeful minds to the duties of this day, confident that with thy help we can fashion something good out of whatever the day may bring; for thy mercies' sake. Amen.

— *New Every Morning, Revised*

69   O GOD, whose Son our Savior labored for his daily bread, that he might be free to serve others: Help me to find happiness and meaning in my work, and to do it with integrity, for the sake of myself and those who depend upon me, as well as for the larger good of many others. Give me respect for and understanding of my employers and fellow-workers, and a deepening sense of our mutual needs; for Jesus Christ's sake. Amen.   — *M. H. S.*

70   O GOD, who hast bound us together in this bundle of life: Give us grace to understand how our lives depend upon the courage, the industry, the honesty, and the integrity of our fellowmen, that we may be mindful of their needs, grateful for their faithfulness, and faithful in our responsibilities to them; through Jesus Christ our Lord. Amen.

— *Reinhold Niebuhr*

71   O GOD, our Father, we thank thee for the trust of our work; for all success in it which has encouraged us, and for all failure, through which we have learnt to do better. Make our work this day, we beseech thee, to be full of the spirit of service. Make it beautiful, by love and honesty, by thoroughness and courtesy. So may our daily work help to bring in thy kingdom; through Jesus Christ our Lord. Amen.

— A Book of Prayers for Schools

72   LORD of all mercy, whose wisdom hath appointed us to our particular places in this life: Strengthen in us such understanding of our spiritual destiny that we may do our work with integrity. Fulfill our relationships with one another in forgiveness and faith, and in all things walk humbly with thee, from whom nothing is hid. Grant us at all times a remembrance of Jesus Christ our Lord, that we may fashion our thoughts in his spirit and our deeds in his love. Amen.

— Samuel H. Miller

73   SET before our minds, O heavenly Father, the example of our Lord Jesus Christ, who when he was upon earth found joy in doing the will of him who sent him, and in finishing his work. When many are coming and going, and there is little quiet, give us grace to remember him who knew neither impatience of spirit nor confusion of work, but in the midst of all his labors kept a tranquil heart, at leisure from itself to serve and sympathize. Amen.

— John Charles Vaughan

74   O GOD, we thank you for the gifts of leisure and
recreation that lighten the load of our daily work:
for joy in the wonders of your creation;
for healthful games and sports;
for times of companionship with family and
friends;
for pursuits of hobbies, crafts, and arts;
for service to our community and those in need;
for extra hours of prayer and spiritual renewal.
For all these gifts of rest and play and other mercies,
accept, O Lord, our grateful praise; through Jesus
Christ our Lord. Amen.

— M. H. S.

75   WITH grateful hearts we thank thee, merciful Father,
for the rest and enjoyment of our holidays; for
sunshine and freedom and pleasant places; for the
happiness of our homes, and the love of those
about us. We pray thee that we may come back
to our daily tasks refreshed, and set about them
with cheerfulness and goodwill, to the best of our
strength and ability; we ask this in the name and
for the love of Jesus Christ our Lord. Amen.

— Lionel James*

76   GIVER of all good things, we thank thee: For health
and vigor; for the air that gives the breath of
life, the sun that warms us, and the good food
that makes us strong; for happy homes and for the
friends we love; for all that makes it good to live.
Make us thankful and eager to repay, by cheerfulness and kindness, and by a readiness to help others
less fortunate than ourselves; for the love of him
who freely gave his life for us, our Savior Jesus
Christ. Amen.

— Prayers for All Occasions*

IV. Personal Gifts and Graces

FAITH

77   O MOST loving Father, who willest us to give thanks for all things, to dread nothing but the loss of thee, and to cast all our care on thee who carest for us: Preserve us from faithless fears and worldly anxieties; and grant that no clouds of this mortal life may hide from us the light of that love which is immortal, and which thou hast manifested unto us in thy Son, Jesus Christ our Lord. Amen.

— William Bright

HOPE

78   ETERNAL God, who rulest the world from everlasting to everlasting: Speak to our hearts when courage fails and love grows cold and there is distress of nations upon the earth. Keep us resolute and steadfast in the things that cannot be shaken. Restore our faith in thine eternal purpose; renew in us the hope which never fails; kindle in us the love which endures all things; and lift up our eyes to the things which are unseen and eternal; through Jesus Christ our Lord. Amen.

— New Every Morning, Revised

LOVE

79   O GOD of patience and consolation: Give us such goodwill, we beseech thee, that with free hearts we may love and serve thee and our brethren; and, having thus the mind of Christ, may begin heaven on earth, and exercise ourselves therein till the day when heaven where love abideth shall seem no strange habitation to us; for Jesus Christ's sake. Amen.

—Christina Georgina Rossetti

JOY

80   O GOD, Author of the world's joy, Bearer of the world's pain: Make us glad that we thy children have inherited the world's burden. Deliver us from the luxury of cheap melancholy; and, at the heart of all our trouble and sorrow, let unconquerable gladness dwell; through our Lord and Savior Jesus Christ. Amen.

— Henry Sylvester Nash*

PATIENCE

81   GOD our Father, look with mercy upon our restless and unpredictable times. Save us from ensnarement in the easy answers and dubious solutions to the complex problems that face our common humanity. Guide us by your Spirit to discern the workings of your purposes; that we may accept with patience and hope the meager offering of our service within your great designs for our world, over which you have made our Savior Jesus Christ Lord of all. Amen.

— M. H. S.

COURAGE

82   O THOU who art heroic love: Keep alive in our hearts that adventurous spirit, which makes men scorn the way of safety, so that thy will be done. For so only, O Lord, shall we be worthy of those courageous souls, who in every age have ventured all in obedience to thy call, and for whom the trumpets have sounded on the farther shore; through Jesus Christ our Lord. Amen.

— The Kingdom, the Power and the Glory

31

GUIDANCE

83   O GOD, by whom the meek are guided in judgment,
and light riseth up in darkness for the godly:
Grant us, in all our doubts and uncertainties, the
grace to ask what thou wouldest have us to do; that
the Spirit of wisdom may save us from all false
choices, and that in thy light we may see light,
and in thy straight path may not stumble; through
Jesus Christ our Lord. Amen.

— William Bright

TRUTHFULNESS

84   O GOD, in whose holy Kingdom there is nothing
that worketh evil or maketh a lie: Help us, we
pray, to guard our words, to keep our promises,
and to speak the truth in love; through Jesus Christ
our Lord. Amen.

— Parish Prayers

DISCERNMENT

85   GOD grant me the serenity to accept the things I
cannot change, the courage to change the things
I can, and the wisdom to distinguish the one from
the other. Amen.

— Reinhold Niebuhr

PERSEVERANCE

86   LOOK upon us and hear us, O Lord our God, and
assist those endeavors to please you which you
yourself have granted us. As you have given us
the first act of will, so give the completion of the
work; and grant that we may be able to finish
what you have granted us the will to begin; through
Jesus Christ our Lord. Amen.

— Mozarabic Liturgy

GENEROSITY

87 MAKE us ever eager, O Lord, to share the good things
that thou dost give us. Grant us such a measure
of thy Spirit that we may find more joy in giving
than in getting. Make us ready to give cheerfully
without grudging, secretly without praise, and in
sincerity without looking for gratitude. For Jesus
Christ's sake. Amen.

— *John Hunter*

INNER PEACE

88 O GOD, whose grace is sufficient for all our need:
Lift us, we pray thee, above our doubts and anxieties into the calm of thy presence; that guarded
by thy peace we may serve thee without fear all
the days of our life; through Jesus Christ our
Lord. Amen.

— *Parish Prayers*

SIMPLICITY OF LIFE

89 TEACH me, good Lord, the virtue of simplicity in
my daily life and habits:
    To pretend no more than I am;
    to desire no more than I need;
    to spend no more than I can afford;
    to consume no more than is just;
that I may be complete yet lacking in nothing,
after the example of my Savior Jesus Christ, who
for our sakes became poor that he might make
many rich. Amen.

— *M. H. S.*

THE SPIRIT OF REVERENCE

90   O THOU in whom we live and move and have our being: Awaken us to thy presence that we may walk in thy world as thy children. Grant us reverence for all thy creation, that we may treat our fellow men with courtesy, and all living things with gentleness; through Jesus Christ our Lord. Amen.

— New Every Morning, Revised

IN TIME OF TEMPTATION

91   O GOD, whom none can love except they hate the thing that is evil, and who willedst by thy Son our Savior to redeem us from all iniquity: Deliver us when we are tempted to look on sin without abhorrence, and let the virtue of his Passion come between us and the enemy of our souls; through the same Jesus Christ our Lord. Amen.

— William Bright

IN TIME OF TROUBLE

92   GRANT, O God, that in this time of testing, I may know thy presence and obey thy will; that with integrity and courage I may accomplish that which thou givest me to do, and endure that which thou givest me to bear; through Jesus Christ my Lord. Amen.

— New Every Morning, Revised*

IN TIME OF SICKNESS

93   O GOD, whether I know or do not know the cause of my present suffering, give me the grace to know and trust your love and care. Strengthen me to bear what I have to bear, and make me thankful for all who minister to my need. If it be your will, restore me to health of body and mind; that, with gratitude for your goodness, I may be a better servant of the needs of others; through Jesus Christ our Lord. Amen.

— M. H. S.

94 BLESSED are they who love you, O God; for they alone lose no one who is dear to them, if all are dear in you, who never can be lost; through Jesus Christ our Lord. Amen. — *Saint Augustine*

95 HEAVENLY Father, by the death and resurrection of your Son our Savior, you have given us a true faith and a sure hope. Uphold us in this time of sorrow for our loved one N., whom you have taken into your eternal keeping, and preserve us from all despair, bitterness, or self-pity. Help us to live as those who believe and trust in the communion of saints, the forgiveness of sins, and the resurrection to life everlasting. Strengthen in us this faith and hope with the assurance of your presence; that we may have courage to face the days to come; for the sake of our Lord Jesus Christ. Amen.

— Adapted from *Various Sources*

A PRAYER FOR ALL TIMES

96 ETERNAL God, who committest to us the swift and solemn trust of life; since we know not what a day may bring forth, but only that the hour of serving thee is always present, may we wake to the instant claims of thy holy will, not waiting for tomorrow, but yielding today. Lay to rest, by the persuasion of thy Spirit, the resistance of our passion, indolence, and fear. Consecrate with thy presence the way our feet may go; and the humblest work will shine, the roughest places be made plain. Lift us above unrighteous anger and mistrust into faith and hope and charity, by a simple and steadfast reliance on thy sure will; and so may we be modest in our time of wealth, patient under disappointment, ready for danger, serene in death. In all things, draw us to the mind of Christ, that thy lost image may be traced again, and thou mayest own us as at one with him and thee. Amen.

— *James Martineau*

V. Intercessions

97   GRACIOUS Father, I humbly beseech thee for thy
      holy Catholic Church: Fill it with all truth, in all
      truth with all peace. Where it is corrupt, purge it;
      where it is in error, direct it; where it is super-
      stitious, rectify it; where anything is amiss, reform
      it; where it is right, strengthen and confirm it;
      where it is in want, furnish it; where it is divided
      and rent asunder, make up the breaches of it, O
      thou Holy One of Israel. Amen.   — *William Laud*

98   O GOD, let thy mercy descend upon the whole
      Church; preserve her in truth and peace, in unity
      and safety, in all storms, and against all tempta-
      tions and enemies; that she, offering to thy glory
      the never-ceasing sacrifice of prayer and thanks-
      giving, may advance the honor of her Lord, and
      be filled with his Spirit, and partake of his glory;
      through Jesus Christ our Lord. Amen.

                                            — *Jeremy Taylor*

99   WE beseech thee, O Lord, to guide thy Church with
      thy perpetual providence; that it may walk warily
      in times of quiet, and boldly in times of trouble;
      through Jesus Christ our Lord. Amen.

                                          — *Missale Francorum*

Its Renewal

100   GOD, our Shepherd, give to the Church a new
      vision and a new charity, new wisdom and fresh
      understanding, the revival of her brightness and
      the renewal of her unity; that the eternal message
      of thy Son, undefiled by the traditions of men,
      may be hailed as the good news of the new age;
      through him who maketh all things new, Jesus
      Christ our Lord. Amen.   — *Percy Dearmer*

101   O GOD, the source of all good gifts, we thank thee for the rich heritage which is ours in thy holy catholic Church. As we realize how much thou hast done for us already, we believe that thou hast also much to give and teach us in our own time. Grant that thy Church may never settle down into mere contentment with the traditions of the past. Grant that it may be alive to all new movements of thy Spirit in our hearts and minds. May it stand always for the removal of injustice and the vindication of righteousness and truth; through Jesus Christ our Lord. Amen.

— A Book of Prayers for Schools*

102   O GOD of unchangeable power and eternal light: Look favorably on your whole Church, that wonderful mystery, and by the effectual working of your perpetual and quiet providence, carry out the salvation of mankind; and let the whole world see and know that things which were cast down are being raised up, and things that have grown old are being made new, and that all things are being brought to their perfection through him by whom all things were made, Jesus Christ our Lord, who lives and reigns with you and the Holy Spirit, one God, for ever and ever. Amen.

— Gelasian Sacramentary

Its Mission

103   O GOD of all the nations of the earth: Remember the multitudes who have been created in your image, and who yet do not know the fullness of your truth and love in the death of your Son Jesus Christ. Grant that by the prayers and labors of your Church they may be delivered from all superstition and unbelief, and brought to worship you through him whom you have sent to be the Resurrection and the Life of all mankind, your Son our Savior Jesus Christ. Amen.

— Saint Francis Xavier*

104 ALMIGHTY God, without whom our labor is but lost: Prosper the work of thy holy Church throughout the world [especially in _____]. Build it upon the foundation other than which no man can lay, Jesus Christ. Defend it from the defilement of worldly motives, unclean hands and the lust of visible success; that in that day when the fire shall prove each one's work of what sort it is, ours may abide, and we, thy laborers, have praise of thee; through the same Jesus Christ our Lord. Amen.   — *Charles Henry Brent* *

105 O GOD, who hast blessed us with the knowledge of the gospel of Christ: make us glad to give of ourselves and of our possessions to carry his gospel to peoples and nations who lack what we have had. Cleanse us from all false pride of race and blood, from self-complacency, and from indifference to the hunger of any human soul. Teach us that life can nowhere find fulfilment except in Christ, and that in our universal need of him we are one with all mankind. And this we ask in the name of him who died for the whole world, and who only in a world redeemed can manifest his risen life. Amen.   — *Walther Russell Bowie* *

106 O ETERNAL God, who art leading us all by new ways which we know not: Grant us the adventurous spirit. Make us willing to attempt new tasks and face new ways, as we seek together thy Kingdom and righteousness. Bestow upon us the gift of love, which believeth all things, hopeth all things, and endureth all things; and so inspire our worship of thee and our service of our fellows that there may be raised, upon the ruins which sin and strife have made, the city whose builder and maker is God. And unto thee, Father, Son and Holy Spirit, shall be praise and honor and dominion, now and for ever. Amen.

— *Edward Arthur Burroughs*

107   O LORD Jesus Christ, who didst pray for thy disciples
that they might be one, even as thou art one with
the Father: Draw us to thyself, that in common
love and obedience to thee we may be united to
one another, in the fellowship of the one Spirit,
that the world may believe that thou art Lord, to
the glory of God the Father. Amen.

                            — *William Temple*

108   O GOD, who didst make the Gospel for a united
Church: Let not our misunderstandings of its
message obstruct thy saving work. Show us
wherein we are sectarian or contentious in spirit,
and give us grace to confess our faults, that we
may become more worthy to bind up the Church's
wounds. Help us to place truth above our con-
ception of it, and joyfully to recognize the presence
of thy Holy Spirit wherever he may choose to dwell;
and so endue us with the mind of Christ, that in
him we may all become one. Amen.

                       — *Charles Henry Brent* *

109   ALMIGHTY God, in whom is calmness, peace and
concord: Heal thou the divisions which separate
thy children from one another, and enable them
to keep the unity of the spirit in the bond of peace.
While there are diversities of knowledge and of
faith, and we cannot all be of the same mind, may
we be made one in brotherly love, and in devotion to thy holy will. Deliver us from all blindness
and prejudice, from all clamor and evil speaking,
that by the charity of our temper and thought and
life, we may show forth the power and beauty of
the religion we profess, to the glory of thy holy
Name. Amen.

                               — *John Hunter*

For the Persecuted

110 GIVE strength and courage, O God, by your Holy Spirit to all who bear reproach or suffer for the Name of our Lord Jesus Christ. Turn the hearts of their oppressors and persecutors; and grant that their testimony may avail for the conversion of many. Keep them steadfast in hope and serene in your peace. Whether in life or in death, number them among your confessors and martyrs who loved not their lives unto death, for the sake of him who died for us all, that we might have everlasting life in glory, our Savior Jesus Christ. Amen.

— M. H. S.

For Those Who Have Gone Astray

111 HEAVENLY Father, whose glory it is always to have mercy: Be gracious, we pray, to all who have erred and gone astray from your holy Word, and bring them in steadfast faith to receive and hold fast your unchangeable truth; through Jesus Christ our Lord. Amen.

— Services for Trial Use
[*Common Service Book of the Lutheran Church,* 1917*]

For the Jewish People

112 O GOD, the God of Abraham and of Isaac and of Jacob: Let your steadfast love be ever with the people of your everlasting covenant. Defend them from all malice, persecution, and affliction. Remember your promises to them of old, and bring them with all who love Jerusalem and mourn for her to the consummation of your Kingdom; through Christ Jesus your Son, who is their Saviour and ours. Amen.

— Adapted from Various Sources

113   POUR out your Spirit abundantly, O God, upon
our Presiding Bishop, N., and upon the Executive
Council and its staff; that they may lead us with
wisdom and courage in the advancement of the
gospel in our land and throughout the world. In
their discouragements give them hope; in their
successes give them comfort; and in all their endeavors may we support them by our prayers and
generosity, with grateful hearts for their service;
through Jesus Christ our Lord. Amen.

— M. H. S.

The Diocese

114   O GOD of all the ages, the God of our fathers,
   we thank you for the heritage and witness
   of all who have gone before us in this Diocese.
Keep us, we pray, faithful to their vision,
   and eager for the promises of your call
   to service in our time.
In the swift and uncertain changes of life today,
   let us not draw back into contentment
   with things that have been,
   for fear of things that may be.
Reveal to us in the face of all people
   the image of our Savior Christ,
   that by the guidance of thy Spirit,
   we may help them to grow with us
   into the full measure and maturity of his manhood,
   in truth, in freedom, and in peace;
Through Jesus Christ our Lord,
   who lives and reigns with you and the Holy Spirit,
   one God, now and for ever. Amen.

— M. H. S.

[Centennial Prayer of the Diocese of Bethlehem]

For the Bishop

115   O GOD, the Pastor and Ruler of your faithful ser-
        vants: Look down in mercy upon your servant
        N., our Bishop [*or,* NN., our Bishops], to whom
        you have given charge over our Diocese; and
        evermore guide, defend, comfort, sanctify and
        save *him;* and grant *him* by your grace so to grow
        and approve *himself* by word and good example,
        that *he,* with the flock committed to *him,* may
        attain to everlasting life; through Jesus Christ our
        Lord. Amen.

                            — *The Cuddesdon Office Book* *

For the Parish

116   O GOD, our heavenly Father, you are ever present
        and praised among your people in every time and
        place: Bestow upon our parish [N.], and the clergy
        [NN.] who minister to us of your Word and Sac-
        raments, the rich blessings of your loving-kindness;
        that we may prove ourselves a people mindful of
        your favor and glad to do your will. Make us alive
        to the opportunities and responsibilities of our
        times; and save us from complacency and from fear
        of new ways. Keep us open to all who need our love
        and fellowship, and inspire us with a vision of a
        world won for Jesus our Lord; that we may pray
        and work, in lowly service and without complaint,
        for the day when your will shall be done on earth as
        it is in heaven; for the sake of our Savior Jesus
        Christ. Amen.

                            — *M. H. S.;* Adapted from *Various Sources*

Peace

117   ALMIGHTY God, from whom all thoughts of truth
and peace proceed: Kindle, we pray thee, in the
hearts of all men, the true love of peace, and
guide with thy pure and peaceable wisdom those
who take counsel for the nations of the earth;
that in tranquillity thy Kingdom may go forward,
till the earth be filled with the knowledge of thy
love; through Jesus Christ our Lord. Amen.

— *Francis Paget*

118   SHOW us, good Lord,
the peace we should seek,
the peace we must give,
the peace we can keep,
the peace we must forego,
and the peace you have given us
in Jesus our Lord. Amen.

— *Contemporary Prayers for Public Worship*

119   O LORD of hosts, from troubled hearts in every
land across the world our prayers ascend to thee.
Cut off from each other by hatred and contempt,
divided by race and language, embittered by envy
and pride, we lift our hands for gifts we will not
receive until we are at peace with one another and
seek thee together in common need. Bring us all
in judgment before Jesus Christ our Lord, whose
great love halted not before shame or death to
forgive in perfect grace those who condemned
him. Bring us at last, lest we come to outer darkness, to kneel in knowledge of our need, and in
such confession humbly to share with all men, in
every condition of servitude and nature, the grace
of thy Holy Spirit, through Jesus Christ our Lord.
Amen.

— *Samuel H. Miller*

120 ALMIGHTY and merciful God, you made the earth fair and plenteous with all things good for the life of your creatures: Deliver us from every waste and abuse of its manifold resources; that we may use them wisely for our own needs and conserve them responsibly for those who will come after us, to your honor and praise; through Jesus Christ our Lord. Amen.

— M. H. S.

121 O GOD, from whose unfailing bounty we draw our life and all that we possess: Forgive our pride and self-sufficiency. Touch us with compassion for the millions in all the world who are starving and destitute. As thou hast given us the knowledge which can produce plenty, so give us also the wisdom to bring it within the reach of all; through Jesus Christ our Lord. Amen.

— *New Every Morning, Revised*

122 O HOLY Wisdom of our God, enlighten all men of science who search out the secrets of thy creation, that their humility before nature may be matched by reverence towards thee. Save us from misusing their labours, that the forces they set free may enrich the life of man, and that thy name may be hallowed both in the search for truth and in the use of power; through Jesus Christ our Lord. Amen.

— *New Every Morning, Revised*

123   O GOD, who art the lover of justice and peace:
Direct, we beseech thee, the minds and wills of
those who are called to deliberate for the welfare
of the nations and the peace of the world; that
as faithful stewards of the things which belong unto
righteousness, they may have regard to thy laws
and the true welfare of mankind. And so guide
them by thy Holy Spirit, that by word and deed
they may promote thy glory, and set forward
peace and mutual goodwill among men; through
Jesus Christ our Lord. Amen.

— The Prayer Manual

124   TEACH us, O Lord, to see other lands and people
by the light of the faith we profess; that we may
check in ourselves all ungenerous judgments, all
presumptuous claims; that being ever ready to
recognize the needs and rightful claims of other
nations we may do whatever in us lies to remove
old hatreds and rivalries, and to hasten new understandings, that each may bring his tribute of
excellence to the treasury of our common humanity;
through Jesus Christ our Lord. Amen.

— Acts of Devotion *

OUR COUNTRY

125   O GOD, whose truth is the only foundation of all
nations: Pour out your Spirit, we pray, upon our
country; that, in honor of your Name and in obedience to your laws, we may be a source of wisdom
and strength, of order and integrity, throughout
the world. Amen.

— New Every Morning, Revised *

126   WE give you humble thanks, O God, for calling our nation into being and for leading us to a place of responsibility in the world. Keep us faithful to the high trust you have laid upon us. Deliver us from arrogance, corruption and injustice; and deepen in us the zeal for righteousness that alone exalts a nation. Unite us with all people of good will in a passion for justice, liberty, and peace; that the reign of Christ may be acknowledged and established among us and in all the world, to the glory of your great Name; through Jesus Christ our Lord, who lives and reigns with you and the Holy Spirit, one God, now and for ever. Amen.

— Adapted from *Various Sources*

Those in Authority

127   ALMIGHTY God, the supreme ruler of peoples and nations: Bestow your blessings of wisdom and courage on those who bear the authority of government in our land [especially NN.]; that they may always uphold what is right and follow what is true for the promotion of justice and peace in accordance with your will; through Jesus Christ our Lord. Amen.

— *M. H. S.*

Citizenship

128   MOST gracious God, we give you thanks for this good land in which our heritage is cast: for freedom to worship you, for liberty of speech and peaceful association, for a government in which we share. Keep us ever mindful and careful of these responsibilities laid upon us, and faithful to our trust to guard and protect them for all our people; through him who is the truth that alone can make us free, your Son, Jesus Christ our Lord. Amen.

— *Communion with God**

Social Justice

129 ALMIGHTY God, who hast created man in thine own image: Grant us grace fearlessly to contend against evil, and to make no peace with oppression; and, that we may reverently use our freedom, help us to employ it in the maintenance of justice among men and nations, to the glory of thy holy Name; through Jesus Christ our Lord. Amen.

— *Edward Lambe Parsons*

The Common Good

130 O GOD, we pray for all men and women in their daily vocations of work and labor. Guard them in temptation, protect them from danger, comfort the heavy-laden. Grant to each and everyone a sense of purpose and meaning to their work in service to the common good, a due appreciation for their toil and a just reward for their labor; through Jesus Christ our Lord. Amen.

— *M. H. S.*

The Armed Forces

131 O LORD God of Hosts, stretch forth, we pray thee, thine almighty arm to strengthen and protect the armed forces of our country, in every peril of sea and land and air. Shelter them in the day of battle, and in the time of peace keep them safe from all evil. Endue them ever with loyalty and courage; and grant that in all things they may serve without reproach; through Jesus Christ our Lord. Amen.

— *John Dowden**

132   ALMIGHTY God, our heavenly Father, in whose
hands are the living and the dead: We give thee
thanks for all those thy servants who have laid
down their lives in the service of our country.
Grant to them thy mercy and the light of thy presence, that the good work which thou hast begun
in them may be perfected; through Jesus Christ
thy Son our Lord. Amen.

          — *Book of Common Prayer*

EDUCATION

Schools, Colleges, and Universities

133   LOOK with your favor, O Lord, on all schools,
colleges, and universities of this and other lands.
Bless all who teach and all who learn; and give
them such integrity of heart and mind that they
may possess a true love of learning and a humble
reverence for truth; for the sake of him who is the
way, the truth, and the life, our Savior Jesus
Christ. Amen.

          — Adapted from *Various Sources*

134   GRANT, O Lord, to all students and teachers to
know what is worth knowing, to love what is
worth loving, to praise what is most pleasing to
you, to esteem what is most dear to you, and to
shun whatever is evil in your sight. Give them
grace to discern the things that differ, and to search
for what is according to your will. Amen.

          — *Thomas a Kempis* *

135   O GOD, who through thy Holy Spirit dost illuminate the minds and sanctify the lives of those whom thou dost call to the work of pastors and teachers: Look with thy favor upon all schools for the instruction and discipline of those who are to serve in the ministry of thy Church. Bless those who teach and those who learn, that they may apply themselves with such diligence to the knowledge which is able to make them wise unto salvation, and submit themselves with such ready obedience to the law of thy Son our Savior, that they may fulfill their ministry with joy; through the same Jesus Christ our Lord. Amen.

— *The Scottish Book of Common Prayer* *

The Public Media

136   DIRECT and bless, O Lord, with your wisdom those who in our generation speak where many listen and write what many read; that they may do their part in making the heart of our people wise, its mind sound, and its will righteous; to the honor and glory of your Name. Amen.

— *The Boy's Prayer Book* *

ARTISTS

137   GRACIOUS God, whose whole creation proclaims the beauty of your handiwork in the heavens and in the earth: We thank you that in every age and culture you have inspired men and women with talent and skill in art and craft and music, which have enriched our lives and ennobled our spirits. Glory be to you for these wondrous gifts, through him who makes all things new, your Son our Lord Jesus Christ. Amen.

— *M. H. S.*

138   ALMIGHTY GOD, whose blessed Son Jesus Christ
       went about doing good, and healing all manner of
       sickness and disease among the people: Continue,
       we beseech thee, this his gracious work among us,
       [especially in NN.]. Cheer, heal, and sanctify the
       sick. Grant to the physicians, surgeons, and nurses
       wisdom and skill, sympathy and patience; and
       send down thy blessing on all who labour to pre-
       vent suffering and to forward thy purposes of
       love; through Jesus Christ our Lord. Amen.

— *Book of Common Prayer,* [English Proposed, 1928]*

139   GRANT, we beseech thee, O merciful God, to all who
       minister healing and comfort to the sick and suf-
       fering thy protection in the way of duty, strength
       and patience, tenderness and love; and may they
       faithfully serve thee in their office for the love of
       thee; through Jesus Christ our Lord. Amen.

— *Prayers of Health and Healing* *

THOSE IN NEED AND TROUBLE

       [This prayer may be said in whole or in
       part. After each petition one may insert
       the names (NN.) of those for whom prayer
       is especially desired.]

140   GOD of mercy and compassion: You bear the afflic-
       tions of your people, and are ever ready to hear our
       prayers for those in any need or trouble, for the
       sake of your Son, who was himself afflicted and
       acquainted with grief:

       For those who are passing through hard times;
       For the aged and infirm who have lost the health and
           strength that once was theirs, and those who have
           no hope of recovery;
       For those who lie in pain or face an operation, and
           those who face illness and suffering bravely;

For all who watch their loved ones suffer; or who have
been bereaved of them;

For those whose sorrow is without the knowledge of
your love;

For those who are addicted and struggle for recovery,
and those who care for them.

For all who are handicapped in life through no fault
of their own and bear permanent injury with courage;

For the crippled, the blind, the deaf, and the dumb;

For the hungry, the homeless, and the destitute;

For those whose livelihood is insecure or who cannot
find work;

For those who are overworked, down-trodden, and
in despair;

For prisoners, captives, and refugees;

For those in mental anguish, and the victims of doubt,
depression, and fear;

For those who are tempted beyond endurance;

For those who are cast down by the evils and sorrows
of the world;

For the persecuted who face trial, torture, and death
for their faith, or their conscientious convictions;

For those indifferent to the needs of others, and who
refuse to share the suffering of the world, seeking
only their comfort and pleasure;

For those whose selfishness brings needless grief to
others;

For all who do not pray, or do not know the consolation of the prayers of others for them;

For all who love their enemies and pray for them.

141   WE thank you, heavenly Father, for all who hallow
suffering; for those whose thought and care for
others leave no room for pity for themselves; for
those whose faith brings light to the dark places
of life; for those whose patience inspires others to
hold on.

142 GRANT, O loving Father, to all who are bound in the mysterious fellowship of suffering the sense of comradeship with others, and the faith and knowledge of your love; and give them your peace which passes understanding, for the sake of our Lord and Savior Jesus Christ. Amen.

— Adapted from *Hugh Martin and Various Sources*

THE ANIMALS

143 O GOD, you created all living things on the face of the earth and gave us dominion over them: Grant that we may be faithful to this trust in the way we treat animals, both wild and tame. Teach us to admire their beauty and to delight in their cunning; to respect their strength and to wonder at their intelligence. Grant that our use of them may be both merciful and wise. So may we lend our voice to their praise of your goodness, which endures for ever. Amen.

— *Charles Philip Price*

144 HEAR our humble prayer, O God, for our friends the animals, especially for those animals that are suffering; for all that are overworked and underfed and cruelly treated; for all wistful creatures in captivity that beat against the bars; for any that are hunted or lost or deserted or frightened; for all that are in pain or dying; for all that must be put to death. We entreat for those who deal with them a heart of compassion, gentle hands, and kind words; that they may share thus the blessing of the merciful. For you, O Lord, will save both man and beast, and great is your loving-kindness. Amen.

— *Russian*

VI. The Christian Year

SUNDAY

145   THIS is the day when the LORD has acted;
let us rejoice and be glad in it!

— Psalm 118:24

146   WE praise and glorify you, O God, for this holy Day:
On the first Day of the world,
you began your marvellous work of creation,
dividing the light from the darkness.
On the first Day of the week,
you raised Jesus your Son from the dead,
and brought new life and immortality to light.
On the Day of Pentecost,
you poured out your Spirit on your Church,
opening to all people the light of the gospel.
On the great and final Day,
you will come in majesty to judge the world,
and bring to light the secrets of all hearts.

O GOD, in our worship of you this day:
Open our lips to sing your praise with joy.
Help us to amend our lives by your Word.
Strengthen us by your Spirit in faith and hope.
Stir our hearts with larger love.
Accept the offering that is pleasing to you.
And renew us in faithful service to our Lord,
Jesus Christ your Son our Savior. Amen.

GLORY to you, eternal Trinity:
Father, Son, and Holy Spirit,
One God, now and always
And throughout all ages. Amen.

— M. H. S.

147 O GOD, who makest us glad with the weekly remembrance of the glorious Resurrection of thy Son
our Lord: Grant us this day such a blessing through
thy worship, that the days which follow it may
be spent in thy favor; through the same Jesus Christ
our Lord. Amen.

— William Bright

148 UNITE us, O Lord, as we worship together this day,
with all your people near and far, who confess
your Name and lift their hearts and minds to you
in praise; that we with them may offer one thanksgiving, partake of one grace, and live in one communion and fellowship, through our one Lord and
Savior Jesus Christ. Amen.

— M. H. S.

149 REMEMBER, O Lord, all who cannot be present this
day in worship with their fellow Christians:
The sick, the infirm, the aged, and all who care
and watch for them;
Those prevented by their work or travel, and those
in places without ministry of your Word and Sac-
raments.
Bind us with them in the unseen fellowship of all
who love you and hope in the coming of the Lord
Jesus.
Remember also, good Lord, those who spurn your
worship through carelessness, indifference, or
hostility; for you also embrace them in your love
and providence, for Jesus' sake. Amen.

— M. H. S.

150   LORD, teach thy people to love thy house best of
       all dwellings, thy Scriptures best of all books, thy
       Sacraments best of all gifts, the communion of
       saints best of all company: and that we may as one
       family and in one place give thanks and adore thy
       glory, help us to keep always thy day, the first of
       of days, holy to thee, our Maker, our Resurrection,
       and our Life, God blessed for ever. Amen.

                                    — *After the Third Collect*
                                    [Adapted from *John Donne*]

                           ADVENT

151   COME, Lord Jesus, come!
           Come in weakness and in power
               to reveal our sin and shame.
           Come, set us free to worship without fear
               and guide us on the road to peace.
           Come, shine on those who dwell in darkness
               and in the shadow of death.
           Come and make all things new,
               in our lives, our labors, and our world.
           Come, save us now in life and death,
               and in the great and final Day.
           Come, Lord Jesus! Alleluia!

                                                — *M. H. S.*

152   ALMIGHTY God, give us grace that we may cast
       away the works of darkness, and put upon us the
       armor of light, now in the time of this mortal life,
       in which thy Son Jesus Christ came to visit us in
       great humility; that in the last day, when he shall
       come again in his glorious majesty, to judge both
       the quick and the dead, we may rise to the life
       immortal, through him who liveth and reigneth
       with thee and the Holy Ghost, now and ever.
       Amen.

                                          — *Thomas Cranmer*

153 PURIFY our consciences, we pray, Almighty God, by your daily visitation, that when your Son our Lord comes, he may find in us a mansion prepared for himself, who lives and reigns with you and the Holy Spirit, one God, now and for ever. Amen.

— *Gelasian Sacramentary*

154 YOUR word is near,
O Lord our God,
your grace is near.
Come to us, then,
with mildness and power.
Do not let us be deaf to you,
but make us receptive and open
to Jesus Christ your son,
who will come to look for us and save us
today and every day
for ever and ever.

— *Huub Oosterhuis*

155 ALMIGHTY God, whose blessed Son Jesus Christ promised to come again to receive his people unto himself: Keep us ever watchful for his glorious appearing. Help us to set our affection on things above, and to live as those who wait for their Lord; that when he shall appear we may be made like unto him, and see him as he is; through the same Jesus Christ our Lord. Amen.

— *The Book of Common Worship, 1946*

156 BRING us, O Lord God, at our last awakening into the house and gate of heaven, to enter into that gate and dwell in that house, where there shall be no darkness nor dazzling but one equal light, no noise nor silence but one equal music, no fears nor hopes but one equal possession, no ends nor beginnings but one equal eternity, in the habitation of thy majesty and thy glory, world without end. Amen.

— *After the Third Collect*
[Adapted from *John Donne*]

157 THE Word became flesh and dwelt among us
    and we beheld his glory,
Glory as of the only-begotten of the Father,
    full of grace and truth.

He was the true light, who lightens
    everyone who comes into the world.
He was in the world, the world was made by him,
    but the world did not know him.

He came to his own people,
    and his own people did not receive him;
But as many as received him and believed on his
    Name,
        he gave them power to be the sons of God.

— John 1:9-12, 14

158 ALMIGHTY and everlasting God, in the incarnation
of your Son our Lord you have revealed the source
and perfection of all true religion: Grant us, we
pray, to have our portion in him who is the one
and only salvation of all mankind, and who lives
and reigns with you and the Holy Spirit, one
God, now and ever. Amen.

— Leonine Sacramentary

159 THIS is the month, and this the happy morn,
Wherein the Son of Heav'n's eternal King,
Of wedded maid and virgin mother born,
Our great redemption from above did bring;
For so the holy sages once did sing,
    That he our deadly forfeit should release,
And with his Father work us a perpetual peace.

— John Milton

160   ALMIGHTY God, you have poured upon us the new
       light of your incarnate Word: Grant, we pray,
       that this light, which is aflame in our hearts by
       faith, may shine forth in our lives; through Jesus
       Christ our Lord, who lives and reigns with you
       and the Holy Spirit, one God, now and for ever.
       Amen.

                            — *Gregorian Sacramentary*

161   LOVE came down at Christmas,
                     Love all lovely, Love divine;
                 Love was born at Christmas,
                     Star and angels gave the sign.

                 Worship we the Godhead,
                     Love incarnate, Love divine;
                 Worship we our Jesus:
                     But wherewith for sacred sign?

                 Love shall be our token,
                     Love be yours and love be mine,
                 Love to God and all men,
                     Love for plea and gift and sign.
                            — *Christina Georgina Rossetti*

162   O GOD, our heavenly Father, we bow in wonder
       at your Gift to us at Christmas, far surpassing
       any gift that we can ever offer. Let us not forget
       those who have no gift but yours, although they
       may not know it. Give us your compassion, that
       we may seek and find them, and give them what
       you have given us, the abundant life and humble
       love of him who made Christmas mean what it is,
       your Son our Savior Jesus Christ. Amen.

                            — *M. H. S.*

163

BEHOLD us bringing
With love and singing
With great joy ringing
And hearts new-made,
The prince, forespoken
By seer and token,
By whom sin's broken
And Death is stayed.

Now by his power
The world will flower,
And hour by hour
His realm increase;
Now men benighted
Will feel them righted,
And loved and lighted
To spirit's peace.

* * *

Our God is wearing
Man's flesh, and bearing
Man's cares, through caring
What men may be;
Our God is sharing
His light and daring
To help men's faring
And set men free.

All you in hearing
Assist our cheering,
This soul unfearing
Who enters earth;
On God relying,
And Death defying,
He puts on dying
That Life have birth.

— *John Masefield*

164　ALMIGHTY and everlasting God, the true Light of your faithful people: You have hallowed this festal time for celebration of the first Gentiles whom you brought to that light. Fill, we pray, the whole world with your glory, and show the clear radiance of your light to all peoples who acknowledge your sway; through Jesus Christ our Lord. Amen.

— Gregorian Sacramentary

165　LORD Jesus Christ, who humbled yourself to receive a baptism of repentance on behalf of sinners, and was forthwith declared to be the beloved Son of your Father: Grant to all who are baptized in your Name to rejoice in their adoption through you as children of your Father, and for your sake as the servants of all. Amen.

— Church of South India*

166　O LORD Jesus Christ, through whose perfect obedience the eternal kingdom once took form on earth and touched our human life with heavenly glory: Teach us the secret of thy humility; that we may ourselves enter into thy kingdom, and pray and work for its triumph in the hearts of all people. Amen.

— New Every Morning, Revised

167　O LORD, who hast set before us the great hope that thy kingdom shall come, and hast taught us to pray for its coming: Give us grace to discern the signs of its dawning, and to work for the perfect day when thy will shall be done on earth as it is in heaven; through Jesus Christ our Lord. Amen.

— Percy Dearmer

168　O GOD, who alone canst uphold the hearts of men: Set us free from vanity and fear, to the end that thine everlasting Gospel may through us reach the world without hurt or hindrance; through our Lord and Savior Jesus Christ. Amen.

— Henry Sylvester Nash

169   MERCIFUL God,
        we confess to you now
        that we have sinned.

    We confess
        the sins that no one knows
           and the sins that everyone knows;
        the sins that are a burden to us
           and the sins that do not bother us
           because we have got used to them.

    We confess our sins as a church.
        We have not loved one another
           as Christ loved us.
        We have not forgiven one another
           as we have been forgiven.
        We have not given ourselves
        in love and service for the world
           as Christ gave himself for us.

    Father, forgive us.
        Send the Holy Spirit to us,
        that he may give us power to live
        as, by your mercy,
        you have called us to live.
    Through Jesus Christ our Lord. Amen.
    — Contemporary Prayers for Public Worship

170   LET us ask the Lord our God for forgiveness
    for the suffering that we cause to others,
    for our forgetfulness and neglect of others,
    for our lack of understanding of each other,
    for speaking ill of other people
    and for the bitterness and spite
    we so often feel towards our fellows,
    for not being able to forgive.
    Let us pray for forgiveness
    of all the sins that men, in their helplessness,
    commit against each other.

    — Huub Oosterhuis

171   We also confess to you, Lord, the unrest of the world,
         to which we contribute and in which we share.
Forgive us that so many of us are indifferent
         to the needs of our fellow men.
Forgive us for our reliance on weapons of terror,
         our discrimination against people of different race,
         and our preoccupation with material standards.
And forgive us Christians for being so unsure
         of our good news and so unready to tell it.
Through Jesus Christ our Lord. Amen.

— Contemporary Prayers for Public Worship

172   O GOD most merciful and holy, forgive us our sins. Forgive us for the sin of blindness which sees so superficially that it sees no sin. More deeply still, forgive the sins that make us blind — the furious haste, weary indifference, hard sophistication, evasive restlessness, covered guilt and the love of comfort. Forgive and save us from that sin of all sins, of denying thee; forgive us for that denial which refuses to face thee; even more for confessing thy name but avoiding thy presence; most of all for coming into thy presence too well protected by self-satisfaction to be humbled by thy glory or meekened by thy grace. Forgive us, O God, and open our eyes that we may repent and be saved, through Jesus Christ our Lord. Amen.

— Samuel H. Miller

173 FORGIVE me, Lord, my sins:
   the sins of my youth,
   the sins of the present;
   the sins I laid upon myself in an ill pleasure,
   the sins I cast upon others in an ill example;
   the sins which are manifest to all the world,
   the sins which I have labored to hide
      from mine acquaintance,
      from mine own conscience,
      and even from my memory;
   my crying and my whispering sins,
   my ignorant sins and my wilful;
   sins against my superiors, equals, servants,
      against my lovers and benefactors,
   sins against myself, mine own body, mine own soul,
   sins against thee, O almighty Father,
      O merciful Son,
      O blessed Spirit of God.
Forgive me, O Lord, through the merits of thine
   Anointed, my Saviour, Jesus Christ. Amen.

— Adapted from *John Donne*
   [*Cuddesdon Office Book*]

174   GRANT us, Almighty God, that by our annual observance of Lenten discipline, we may grow in the knowledge of Christ, and make our lives worthy of his love; for his sake, who lives and reigns with you and the Holy Spirit, one God, for ever and ever. Amen.

— Gelasian Sacramentary

175   THE glory of these forty days
We celebrate with songs of praise;
For Christ, by whom all things were made,
Himself has fasted and has prayed.

Alone and fasting Moses saw
The loving God who gave the law;
And to Elijah, fasting, came
The steeds and chariots of flame.

So Daniel trained his mystic sight,
Delivered from the lions' might;
And John, the Bridegroom's friend, became
The herald of Messiah's name.

Then grant us Lord, like them to be
Full oft in fast and prayer with thee;
Our spirits strengthen with thy grace,
And give us joy to see thy face. Amen.

— Matins Hymn for Lent
[Translated by *Maurice F. Bell*]

176   WE pray to you, O Lord: Support us through the fast we have begun; that, as we observe it with bodily self-denial, so we may fulfill it with inner sincerity of heart; through Jesus Christ our Lord. Amen.

— Gelasian Sacrementary

177

IS this a fast, to keep
    The larder lean?
      And clean
From fát of veals and sheep?

Is it to quit the dish
    Of flesh, yet still
      To fill
The platter high with fish?

Is it to fast an hour,
    Or ragg'd to go
      Or show
A downcast look and sour?

No: 'tis a fast to dole
    Thy sheaf of wheat,
      And meat,
Unto the hungry soul.

It is to fast from strife,
    From old debate
      And hate;
To circumcise thy life.

To show a heart grief-rent;
    To starve thy sin,
      Not bin;
And that's to keep thy Lent.

                — *Robert Herrick*

178   MERCIFUL and faithful High Priest, who didst deign
for us to be tempted of Satan: Make speed to aid
thy servants who are assaulted by manifold temptations; and as thou knowest their several infirmities,
let each one find thee mighty to save; who livest
and reignest with the Father and the Holy Spirit,
one God, now and for ever.

                — *William Bright*

179   LORD, bless to me this Lent.

Lord, let me fast most truly and profitably,
   by feeding in prayer on thy Spirit:
      reveal me to myself
         in the light of thy holiness.

Suffer me never to think
   that I have knowledge enough to need no teaching,
      wisdom enough to need no correction,
      talents enough to need no grace,
      goodness enough to need no progress,
      humility enough to need no repentance,
      devotion enough to need no quickening,
      strength sufficient without thy Spirit;
   lest, standing still, I fall back for evermore.

Shew me the desires that should be disciplined,
   and sloths to be slain.
Shew me the omissions to be made up
   and the habits to be mended.
And behind these, weaken, humble
   and annihilate in me
   self-will, self-righteousness, self-satisfaction,
   self-sufficiency, self-assertion, vainglory.

May my whole effort be to return to thee;
   O make it serious and sincere
   persevering and fruitful in result,
      by the help of thy Holy Spirit
         and to thy glory
            my Lord and my God.

— *Eric Milner-White*

180   O GOD of our salvation, grant us the help of your
grace, that we may approach with joy the remembrance of your mercies, by which you have restored
to us newness of life; through our Lord Jesus Christ.
Amen.

— Gelasian Sacramentary

181   GOD, our heavenly Father:
In this holy week we are unable to forget
how our Lord Jesus Christ glorified you
in his perfect and final obedience to your will;
how he glorified our humanity which he bore,
when he was lifted on the Cross to take away
our sin,

'that we who were dead in our trespasses
might be made alive together with him,
by the forgiveness of our sins;
that the principalities and powers,
which oppress us, might be disarmed
by his triumph over them.'

We bow before this great mystery
of your love and power; and we pray
that as we believe it, so we may receive it;
nor let us resist, against our conscience,
the judgment of its truth and its demand;
and give us now the grace and strength
to accept joyfully the mystery of that Cross;
that we not only worship him there with our lips,
but help him to bear it on our backs;
that he may there reveal to us and to the world
his glory and his peace. Amen.

— M. H. S.

182   ALMIGHTY God, who in the life and teaching of thy Son, hast showed unto us the true way of blessedness; thou hast also showed us, in his sufferings and death, that the path of duty may lead to the cross, and the reward of faithfulness may be a crown of thorns. Give us grace to learn these harder lessons. May we take up our cross and follow Christ in the strength of patience and the constancy of faith; and may we have such fellowship with him in his sorrow that we may know the secret of his strength and peace, and see, even in our darkest hour of trial and anguish, the shining of the eternal light. Amen.

— John Hunter

183   JESUS now hath many lovers of his celestial kingdom:
    but few bearers of his Cross.
He hath many who are desirous of consolation:
    but few of tribulation.
He findeth many companions of his table:
    but few of his abstinence.
All desire to rejoice with him;
    few wish to endure anything for him.
Many follow Jesus to the breaking of bread:
    but few to the drinking of the cup of his Passion.
Many reverence his miracles:
    few follow the shame of his Cross.

— Thomas a Kempis

184   O LORD Jesus Christ, Son of the living God: Grant us of thy tender grace true fellowship with thee in thy sufferings, by abhorring and renouncing the open sins and the secret sins, the little sins and the great sins, which crucify thee afresh; who now livest and reignest with the Father and the Holy Ghost, God, for ever and ever. Amen.

— Eric Milner-White

185   O LOVING Wisdom of the living God, O everlasting
Word and Power of the eternal Father: Grant us
what you have promised; and give us, unworthy
as we are, what you have offered to all alike;
that your passion may be our deliverance and your
death our life, your cross our redemption and your
wound our healing; and that, being crucified with
you, we may by your gift be exalted to your Father
on high, with whom you live and reign with the
Holy Spirit, one God, blessed for evermore. Amen.

— Missale Gallicanum Vetus

186   FATHER of our Lord Jesus Christ: We beseech thee
to engender in us such a living spirit that we may
remember the life and labor of our Lord, not
vainly as a thing long gone, but fruitfully, seeing
in our own days that same incredible love which
revealed in him the glory of thy great grace bearing the cross for our sakes, even as now. Amen.

— Samuel H. Miller

187   LORD God,
        you sent your son into the world
        with no other certainty
        but that he had to suffer and to die.
        He fulfilled his mission to the end.
        And in this way he became
        a source of life and joy.
        We ask you
        to perfect our joy
        and let the world see
        that he is living
        here among us
        everywhere on earth.

— Huub Oosterhuis

188 HAIL! Festal Day! for evermore adored
Wherein God conquered Hell, and upward soared!

The power of Satan crushed, He seeks the skies;
From earth, light, stars, and ocean, anthems rise!

When Death and Hell the human race o'erran,
Thou, man to save, thyself becamest Man.

The Crucified reigns God for evermore;
Their Maker all created things adore.

> — *Venantius Honorius Fortunatus*
> [Translated by *John Mason Neale*]

189 O GOD, who for our redemption gave your only-
begotten Son to the death of the Cross, and by his
glorious Resurrection delivered us from the power
of our enemy: Grant us so to die daily from sin,
that we may evermore live with him in the joy
of his Resurrection; through Jesus Christ our Lord,
who lives and reigns with you and the Holy Spirit,
one God, now and for ever. Amen.

> — *Gregorian Sacramentary*

190 SING, men and angels, sing,
For God our Life and King
Has given us Light and Spring
And morning breaking.
Now may Man's Soul arise
As kinsman to the skies,
And God unseals his eyes
To an awaking.
Sing, creatures, sing; the dust
That lives by lure and lust
Is kindled by the thrust
Of life undying;

This Hope our Master bare
Has made all fortunes fair,
And Man can on and dare
His death defying.

After the winter snows
A wind of healing blows,
And thorns put forth a rose
And lilies cheer us;
Life's everlasting Spring
Hath robbed Death of his sting,
Henceforth a cry can bring
Our Master near us.

— *John Masefield*

191   DEAR Father,
This is the best day of the whole year —
the best day of all time.
For on Easter Day we find that Jesus, who was
dead, is alive again, and that those who put
their trust in him shall not be swept away by
death, but shall have eternal life.
Make us willing and able to change our old ways
of thinking and speaking and doing into Easter
ways; so that how we behave may bear out what
we believe, and so that Christ's new creation
may become in us not just a hope but a fact;
Through the same Jesus Christ our Lord, who
lives and reigns with you, our Father, and the
Holy Spirit, one God for ever and ever. Amen.

— *Contemporary Prayers for Public Worship**

192   JESUS holds his priesthood permanently, because he
      continues for ever. Consequently he is able for all
      time to save those who draw near to God through
      him, since he always lives to make intercession for
      them.

      For Christ has entered, not into a sanctuary made
      with hands, a copy of the true one, but into heaven
      itself, now to appear in the presence of God on
      our behalf.

      — *Hebrews 7:24-25, 9:24*

193   OUR Life himself came down to earth and took away
      our death. He slew it with the abundance of his own
      life, called us with a voice as of thunder to return
      hence to him, to that secret place from whence he
      had come forth to us — calling us by his words
      and deeds, by his death, his life, his descent to the
      dead and his ascent to heaven — calling us to
      return to him. He departed from our sight that
      we might turn back into our hearts and find him
      there. Though he departed, lo! he is still here.
      He did not will to be with us long, yet he did not
      leave us. He went back to the place from which
      he had never left, for the world was made through
      him. He was in the world, and he came into the
      world to save sinners.

      — *Saint Augustine, Confessions, iv. 12*

194   AND have the bright immensities
               Received our risen Lord,
           Where light-years frame the Pleiades
               And point Orion's sword?
           Do flaming suns his footsteps trace
               Through corridors sublime,
           The Lord of interstellar space
               And Conqueror of time?

The heav'n that hides him from our sight
  Knows neither near nor far:
An altar candle sheds its light
  As surely as a star;
And where his loving people meet
  To share the gift divine,
There stands he with unhurrying feet
  There heav'ly splendors shine.

— Howard Chandler Robbins

195   BE present, O Lord, to our prayers; for as we believe the Savior of mankind is seated with you in your majesty, so may we discern that, according to his promise, he abides with us to the end of the world; through Jesus Christ our Lord. Amen.

— Leonine Sacramentary

196   O THOU merciful and loving High Priest, who hast passed within the veil and art in the presence of the Father: Help us with thy mighty intercession, that, our unworthiness being clothed upon with thy perfect righteousness, we may stand accepted in the day of thy coming; who livest and reignest with the Father and the Holy Spirit, one God, for ever and ever. Amen.

— Henry Alford

197   ALMIGHTY and everlasting God, who hast willed to restore all things in thy well-beloved Son, the King and Lord of all: Mercifully grant that all the peoples and nations, divided and wounded by sin, may be brought under the gentle yoke of his most loving rule; who with thee and the Holy Spirit liveth and reigneth, ever one God, now and for ever. Amen.

— Collect for the Feast of Christ the King
[Translation, *Edward C. Trenholme, S.S.J.E.*]

198

COME down, O Love divine,
Seek thou this soul of mine,
And visit it with thine own ardor glowing;
O Comforter, draw near,
Within my heart appear,
And kindle it, thy holy flame bestowing.

O let it freely burn,
Till earthly passions turn
To dust and ashes in its heat consuming;
And let thy glorious light
Shine ever on my sight,
And clothe me round, the while my path illuming.

Let holy charity
Mine outward vesture be,
And lowliness become mine inner clothing;
True lowliness of heart,
Which takes the humbler part,
And o'er its own shortcomings weeps with loathing.

And so the yearning strong,
with which the soul will long,
Shall far outpass the power of human telling;
For none can guess its grace,
Till he become the place
Wherein the Holy Spirit makes his dwelling.

— *Bianco da Siena*
[Translated, *Richard Frederick Littledale*]

199   O GOD, who through the mystery of today's festival hallow your universal Church in every race and nation: Pour out the gifts of your Holy Spirit throughout the length and breadth of the world; that the work of your divine grace, which was first wrought in the preaching of the gospel, may now also be poured out within the hearts of all believers, through Jesus Christ our Lord. Amen.

— Gelasian Sacramentary

200   ALMIGHTY and everlasting God, in the fullness of today's mystery you have brought to completion the secret work of the Paschal festival: Grant, we pray, that we who were made your adopted children may also obtain your peace, which our Lord Jesus Christ left to us when he returned to you in everlasting glory. Amen.

— Leonine Sacramentary

201   O HOLY Spirit,
      Giver of light and life:
Impart to us thoughts higher than our own thoughts,
    and prayers better than our own prayers,
    and powers beyond our own powers;
that we may spend and be spent
      in the ways of love and goodness,
    after the perfect image
      of our Lord and Savior Jesus Christ. Amen.

— Eric Milner-White

202   O GOD, who didst send thy Word to speak in the Prophets and live in thy Son, and appoint thy Church to be witness of divine things in all the world: Revive the purity and deepen the power of its testimony; and through the din of earthly interests and the storm of human passions, let it make the still small voice of thy Spirit inly felt. Nearer and nearer may thy Kingdom come from age to age; and by the cleansing of thy Spirit, make this world a fitting forecourt to that sanctuary not made with hands, where our life is hid with Christ, O God, in thee. Amen.

75

— John Hunter*

203   O ETERNAL God, Father, Son, and Holy Spirit:
Grant that in the majesty of all creation we may
behold thy power that upholds us, in the face of
Jesus Christ thy love that seeks and saves us, and
in the new life within our souls thy Spirit kindling
in us; that so even to our littleness thine infinite
wonder may be revealed, O blessed Triune God.
Amen.

— Walter Russell Bowie

THE TRANSFIGURATION

204   O GOD, who before the passion of thine only-
begotten Son didst reveal his glory upon the holy
mount: Grant unto us thy servants that, in faith
beholding the light of his countenance, we may be
strengthened to bear the cross, and be changed
into his likeness from glory to glory; through the
same Jesus Christ our Lord. Amen.

— Book of Common Prayer, [English Proposed, 1928]

SAINTS' DAYS

205   O GOD, who hast brought us near to an innumerable
company of Angels, and to the spirits of just men
made perfect: Grant us during our pilgrimage to
abide in their fellowship, and in our Country to
become partakers of their joy; through Jesus Christ
our Lord. Amen.

— William Bright

206   ALMIGHTY and everlasting God, who dost enkindle
the flame of thy love in the hearts of the saints:
Give to our hearts the same faith and power of
love; that, as we rejoice in their triumphs, we
may profit by their examples; through Jesus Christ
our Lord. Amen.

— The Gothic Missal

207 ETERNAL God, in whom do live the spirits of those who depart hence: We remember with quiet and grateful hearts our brethren and sisters who from the beginning of the world have pleased thee in their several generations, and have now found their everlasting rest and home in thee. Mercifully grant that their example and memory may stir us to a better life; that when for us the night cometh when no man can work, we may be counted worthy to join their fellowship in that world where peace and love are perfect and immortal. Amen.

— *John Hunter*

Saint Mary

208 O CHRIST, our God Incarnate, whose Virgin Mother was blessed in bearing thee, but still more blessed in keeping thy word: Grant us, who honor the exaltation of her lowliness, to follow the example of her devotion to thy will; who livest and reignest with the Father and the Holy Spirit, one God, now and for ever. Amen.

— *William Bright*

Saint John the Baptist

209 ALMIGHTY God, by whose providence your servant John the Baptist was wonderfully born to be the forerunner of our Savior Jesus Christ: Give us grace to repent according to his preaching, and to turn to you with all our hearts; that we may be ready for that day when the glory of the Lord shall be revealed; through Jesus Christ our Lord, who lives and reigns with you in the unity of the Holy Spirit, one God, now and ever. Amen.

— *Services for Trial Use*

Apostles

210   O ALMIGHTY God, who hast built thy Church upon the foundation of the Apostles and Prophets, Jesus Christ himself being the head cornerstone: Grant us so to be joined together in unity of spirit by their doctrine, that we may be made an holy temple acceptable unto thee; through the same Jesus Christ our Lord. Amen.

— Book of Common Prayer

Martyrs

211   HEAVENLY Father, whose Son our Savior will come again to be glorified in his saints: We give you thanks for all your martyrs in every age, who have loved not their lives unto death [and especially N.]. Grant that we, who give praise for their witness, may never be ashamed to give an account of the faith that is in us, for the sake of our Lord Jesus Christ, who gave his life for us that we might live in him. Amen.

— M. H. S.

Missionaries

212   ALL glory to you, heavenly Father, for those who in every age have been faithful to their Lord's commission, and have gone to the ends of the earth to proclaim the joyful news of salvation; to bring light to those who dwelt in darkness and the shadow of death [especially your servant N.].

We thank you for all who endured loneliness, danger, and disrepute for the sake of the gospel; for those who gave their lives for the faith, and whose converts sealed their witness with their blood.

Glory to you, Lord God, for the innumerable company out of every kindred and nation and tongue, who now praise the Name of your Son Jesus Christ, the Savior of the world. Amen.

— Adapted from Divine Service

213   O GOD, our Shepherd, you gave us in your servant
      N. a faithful pastor of your flock, constant and
      unwearied in nourishing them with the truth of
      your Word and the grace of your Sacraments:
      Grant that we may follow the example and teach-
      ing of his holy life, and gain the maturity and
      stature of the fullness of Christ our Lord and
      Savior. Amen.

                    — Adapted from *Various Sources*

Teachers

214   O GOD of truth, by whose Holy Spirit is given to
      some the word of wisdom, to others the word of
      knowledge, and to others the word of faith: We
      praise your Name for the gifts of grace imparted
      to your servant N.; and we pray that by *his* teach-
      ing we may know you, the only true God, and
      Jesus Christ whom you have sent, and who now
      lives and reigns with you and the Holy Spirit,
      one God, for evermore. Amen.

                          — *Services for Trial Use* *

THE COMMUNION OF SAINTS

215   LET us commemorate before the Lord
            all who have left this world
                and have died in the faith.
      May God bestow on them the crown of life
            in the Day of resurrection,
      and judge them worthy with the righteous
            who have pleased him
      to enter into the joy of their Master.

Let us recall before the Lord
    all his servants and witnesses in times past,
    particularly Abraham, the father of all believers,
    Moses, Samuel and David, Elijah, Isaiah, Jeremiah
        and all the prophets,
    John the Baptist, the Forerunner,
    Peter and Paul, John and James, and the other
        apostles,
    Stephen the first martyr,
    Mary the Mother of the Lord,
    And all the saints, martyrs, and teachers of the
        Church, in every age and in every land.
May the Lord God, in his mercy
    give us with them hope in his salvation,
    and in the promise of eternal life in his Kingdom.

                    — The Taizé Liturgy 1959

VII. Times of Renewal

NEW YEAR'S DAY

216 FATHER, as the old year ends and a new year begins, forgive us for the failures of the vanished days, and bless us in whatever we have truly striven for in days that do not die. Keep us from vain regrets, and let us face forward in the light of the best that we have learned. Purge our hearts both of shallow self-confidence and of cowardly fears, so that we may know that without thee we can do nothing but that in thee all things are possible; through Jesus Christ our Lord. Amen.

— Walter Russell Bowie

217 ETERNAL God, who makest all things new, and abidest for ever the same: Grant us to commence this year in thy faith, and continue it in thy favor; that being guided in all our doings, and guarded in all our days, we may spend our lives in thy service, and finally, by thy grace, attain the glory of everlasting life; through Jesus Christ our Lord. Amen.

— W. E. Orchard

PASCHAL TIME

[Easter]

218 ALMIGHTY and everlasting God, who established the new covenant of reconciliation in the Paschal mystery of Christ: Grant that all who have been reborn into the fellowship of his Body, may show forth in their lives what they profess by their faith; through Jesus Christ our Lord. Amen.

— Gregorian Sacramentary

219   O LORD Jesus Christ, who didst say to thine Apostles, "Come ye apart into a desert place and rest awhile": Grant to us, thy servants, so to seek thee whom our souls desire to love, that we may both find thee and be found of thee. And grant such love and wisdom to accompany the words that shall be spoken in thy Name, that they may not fall to the ground, but may be helpful in leading us onward through our pilgrimage to the rest that remaineth to the people of God. Amen.

— Richard Meux Benson*

220   COME quietly, O God, and still our noisy, boisterous, stormy selves;
come with power, and cast out the many devils which divide us and torment us with their fears and contradictions;
come with grace, and exalt our dreams and deeds with knowledge of thine ever-present companionship amid this world's varied circumstance;
come with love, and bind us in the fellowship of the forgiven with thy children everywhere, in Christ's Name. Amen.

— Samuel H. Miller

[For use before the Holy Eucharist, or the Sacrament of Reconciliation; or for personal devotion]

221 1. Personal Living: Do I? —

Live every day in thankfulness for God's many blessings, with trust in his never-failing goodness and care for me, and his power to turn evil into good.

Grow in my love for God, and thereby in my love for others and for myself.

Take time daily for prayer and meditation, and be diligent in corporate worship with my fellow Christians.

Apply myself regularly to study and learn the meaning of my faith and how it applies to my everyday life and behavior.

Make my work an offering to God, for his honor and the benefit of others.

Treat all persons, whatever their condition or character, with courtesy and respect, seeking always the best in them, and seeing in them the face of Christ.

Try never to use or manipulate others to my own advantage, nor put them down for any cause.

Endeavor always to be truthful and honest, without deceit or hypocrisy.

Give up to God the pleasures of anger, grumbling, and self-pity.

Thank God for the spiritual growth that can come through suffering, disappointment, and frustration.

Reverence the good things of God's creation, and check all tendencies of waste, extravagance, and self-indulgence.

Use my natural gifts and talents responsibly, and without fretting over my limitations.

Learn to accept honest criticism, and make no return of insult or neglect from others, knowing God's acceptance of me, even in my failures.

Live each day without anxiety or fear of misfortune, and trust God's mercy to keep me in the hour of death.

2. Social Living: Do I? —

Love each one of my family, rejoice in their gifts and successes, comfort them in sorrows and failures; listen to them and share their interests; deny myself for their welfare.

Enjoy giving hospitality to relatives, neighbors, friends, strangers, and those who are lonely.

Accept gladly menial tasks that help others who are burdened and in need.

Take my part in work and programs for the betterment of my community and the support of those who are poor, helpless, and oppressed.

Labor to root out from my own life and from my community and nation, and, so far as possible, from the world of men and women, prejudice and discrimination against all sorts and conditions of people.

Try to understand current events with Christian discernment, and thereby exercise my rights and responsibilities as a citizen.

Respect, and pray regularly for, the leaders of the nations and all who work for justice and peace.

Seek to reconcile those who are in strife and enmity, without self-righteousness or arrogance.

Lay before God constantly the sins of our common humanity, with penitence for my own share in them, for his forgiveness and healing power.

3. Church Living. Do I? —

  Support the mission of the Church at home and abroad by prayer, work, and adequate stewardship of my time, talents, and means.

  Commend by my conversation and behavior the Christian faith, and make myself expendable for the gospel.

  Help and encourage others to attend faithfully with me the public worship of my Church.

  Promote understanding, peace, and a forgiving spirit among church people who are angry or disgusted either with what the Church is doing or with what it is not doing.

  Speak always respectfully and charitably of those, whether clergy or lay, who hold responsible positions of leadership in the Church.

  Keep myself informed about, and cherish the many good things that dedicated and unselfish people are doing to promote the spread of God's Kingdom — in the parish, the diocese, the national Church, and the wider mission of God's people throughout the world.

  Appreciate the faith, character, and devotion of Christians of other traditions than my own; and pray with them for the Holy Spirit to direct, purify, and reunite us in one Body of faith and hope and love.

Adapted from *"In Newness of Life"*
[Associated Parishes, Inc.]

VIII. The Holy Eucharist

THE MEANING OF THE LORD'S SUPPER

222   OUR Lord celebrated his last act with his disciples in his earthly life, and his first act with them in his risen life at a common meal, in and through which he gave himself. "He was made known to them in the breaking of the bread" (*Luke 24:35*). So he continues, throughout all time, to make the grace and power of his presence known to those who believe in him, and who love and serve him, wherever they may be in the world.

The Lord's Supper is thus the unique and distinctive act of Christians that binds them by word and deed in a continual, living relationship with their Redeemer and Lord, and through him one with another. As the peculiar observance of the Church of Jesus Christ, it is both sign and sacrament of its unity, its mission, and its promise.

The many facets of meaning joined together in the Lord's Supper cannot be comprehended by any simple definition, much less by a single title. The full reality of the Church — past, present, and future — is exhibited in it.

The Supper is a memorial feast that celebrates what Jesus Christ accomplished for the salvation of the world in his sacrificial life and death, and in his triumph over sin and death. In obedience to his command, "Do this in remembrance of me" (*1 Corinthians 11:24-25*), Christian disciples recall with joy and thanksgiving the wondrous once-for-all gift of his redeeming work and promise of eternal life. They contemplate its inexhaustible mystery and benefit, and pledge themselves anew in commitment to its gospel.

The Supper is no mere commemoration of a past and glorious event. Jesus Christ lives and abides with his Church for ever. "Where two or three are gathered in my name, there am I in the midst of them" (*Matthew 18:20*). The presence of Christ among his own, here and now, in grace and power and judgment, presiding and serving at his banquet table, is an inescapable reality for all who meet him in the Supper. It is, in fact, a holy communion. This living encounter evokes penitence, faith, love, joy. It mediates forgiveness, reconciliation, hope, encouragement, consolation, and spiritual strength. The Supper is Christ's immediate means of grace — making up what is lacking, supporting what is weak, confirming what is good, and empowering what is needful.

The Supper is also a real participation in the final end of the redeemed — that Messianic banquet which the Lord prepares and makes ready in his Kingdom. "Blessed are those who are invited to the marriage supper of the Lamb" (*Revelation 19:9*). The new heaven and the new earth find anticipation here in this act, because it reveals the true end of our calling to reconciliation, obedience, and peace. Holy Communion is indeed the final purpose of God not only for all mankind but for all creation. To know that communion is to know the reality of the world to come. In the Supper our ascended Lord lifts up his embattled followers on earth into union with the triumphant hosts of heaven in adoration of the Holy.

— *M. H. S.*

223   The Son of Man came not that we might minister
to Him, but that He might minister to us, and this
should be in our minds as we come to keep the feast.
There is much that we can do for Christ; and the
Christian life in its practical aspects is much con-
cerned with Christian duty and Christian service. We
have to carry on His work, commend His Gospel,
fill up even His sufferings as St. Paul declared. We
have to show His love by the love of our lives. When
on earth He submitted to be ministered unto. Men
and women loved Him in the days of His pilgrimage
and tended Him. Martha and other holy women
sometimes cumbered themselves with much serving
of Him, and found delight in doing it. He accepted
hospitality, went out to the little home in Bethany,
where He would rest and be served. Peter would be
proud to wash His feet. The disciples would minister
to Him when and where they could. Loving women
went to His sepulchre to anoint His body, and give
it the last sweet ministrations. But He did not come
for all this — not to be ministered unto, but Himself
to minister.

We also in our measure can minister to Him. He
said that a cup of cold water to one of His little ones
was given to Him. Whatever we do in His spirit for
men is done for Him. Many a ministry of the Lord
is possible to us. If we are His disciples we will seek
to serve Him in the ways that He loved to serve.
Inevitable as this is and needful as it is both for our
own sake and for the sake of others, yet He did not
come that we might do this for Him. He came to do
something for us. It is possible for us to be so taken up
with all our religious activities that we may forget
to wait to let Christ do His work upon ourselves.
Our Communion season comes to us, calling a halt,
reminding us that it is true for us also, as for the
disciples of old, that the Son of Man came not to
be ministered unto but to minister. It is good to cease
from serving sometimes, and let Christ serve us.

This is one of the chief lessons of our holy Communion. We are not hosts here at all, taking charge and dispensing benefits. We come as guests simply. We bring nothing to the feast except need, nothing except hunger and thirst after righteousness. We do not make the provision: we only come to partake. He is the Giver and the Gift. He prepares the feast, invites us all unworthy, omits not one gracious act of courtesy, breaks the bread, gives us the wine of His love. The Son of Man came to minister, let Him minister. It is His pleasure to serve, let Him serve. It is His joy to give, let Him give.

— *Hugh Black*

224   LORD, this is thy feast,
              prepared by thy longing,
              spread at thy command,
              attended at thine invitation,
              blessed by thine own Word,
              distributed by thine own hand,
              the undying memorial of thy sacrifice
                    upon the Cross,
              the full gift of thine everlasting love,
              and its perpetuation till time shall end.

    LORD, this is the Bread of heaven,
              Bread of life,
              that, whoso eateth, never shall hunger more.
              And this the Cup of pardon, healing,
                    gladness, strength,
              that, whoso drinketh, thirsteth not again.
    So may we come, O Lord, to thy Table;
              Lord Jesu, come to us.

                            — *Eric Milner-White*

225   SEARCH us deeply, O God, that remembering Jesus Christ our Lord, our minds and hearts may be cleansed of all insincerities, of self-righteous poses and dubious devotions. Show us the great glory of him who lived so faithfully and died so humbly in revealing thy grace. Grant us no peace in idle meditations but thrust us by thy Holy Spirit into the very life of our time and town, that with seeing eyes and open souls we may entertain the Lord of life and if need be carry the cross of the Son of Man. Amen.

                          — *Samuel H. Miller*

226 HERE, O my Lord, I see thee face to face;
  Here would I touch and handle things unseen;
Here grasp with firmer hand th'eternal grace,
  And all my weariness upon thee lean.

Here would I feed upon the bread of God;
  Here drink with thee the royal wine of heaven;
Here would I lay aside each earthly load,
  Here taste afresh the calm of sin forgiven.

I have no help but thine; nor do I need
  Another arm save thine to lean upon;
It is enough, my Lord, enough indeed;
  My strength is in thy might, thy might alone.

* * *

This is the hour of banquet and of song;
  This is the heavenly table spread for me;
Here let me feast, and, feasting, still prolong
  The brief, bright hour of fellowship with thee.

Too soon we rise; the symbols disappear;
  The feast, though not the love, is past and gone;
The bread and wine remove; but thou art here,
  Nearer than ever, still my shield and sun.

Feast after feast thus comes and passes by,
  Yet, passing, points to the glad feast above,
Giving sweet foretaste of the festal joy,
  The Lamb's great bridal feast of bliss and love.

— Horatius Bonar

227   O GOD, set our hearts at liberty from the service of
ourselves, and let it be our meat and drink to do
thy will; through Jesus Christ our Lord. Amen.

— Henry Sylvester Nash

228   GOD be in my head,
           and in my understanding.
         God be in mine eyes,
           and in my looking.
         God be in my mouth,
           and in my speaking.
         God be in my heart,
           and in my thinking.
         God be at mine end,
           and at my departing.

— Sarum Primer

229   THANKS be to thee, my Lord Jesus Christ,
for all the benefits which thou hast given me,
for all the pains and insults
which thou hast borne for me.

O most merciful Redeemer, Friend, and Brother,
may I know thee more clearly,
love thee more dearly,
and follow thee more nearly,
for ever and ever. Amen.

— Saint Richard of Chichester

230 WE have finished and perfected, O Christ our God,
   so far as we are able, the Mystery you have or-
   dained:
   We have celebrated the memorial of your death;
   We have seen the image of your resurrection;
   We have been filled with your unending life;
   We have enjoyed your inexaustible delight,
      of which may you be pleased to account us worthy
      of the world to come; by the grace of your eternal
      Father, and of your holy, good, and life-giving
      Spirit, now and ever, and unto the ages of ages.
      Amen.

                                    — *Liturgy of Saint Basil*

231 REMEMBER, O Lord, what you have wrought in us,
   and not what we deserve; and as you have called
   us to your service, make us worthy of our calling;
   through Jesus Christ our Lord. Amen.

                                    — *Leonine Sacramentary* *

232 FOR bread broken in the glory of a common joy;
   for truth living beyond the barriers of time; for
   fellowship made out of an understanding of eternal
   things; for humble circumstance and simple deed
   in which the ineffable miracle of love is perfectly
   revealed; for mysteries by which we have been
   exalted and for knowledge by which we have
   been humbled; for souls in whose living we have
   seen no death, and for those who, having died,
   live for ever — we give thee thanks with great
   rejoicing, O God our Lord. Amen.

                                    — *Samuel H. Miller*

233　O MOST gracious and eternal God, the helper of the helpless, the comforter of the comfortless, the hope of the afflicted, the bread of the hungry, the drink of the thirsty, and the Savior of all them that wait upon thee:

I bless and glorify thy Name, and adore thy goodness, and delight in thy love, that thou hast once more given me the opportunity of receiving the greatest favor which I can receive in this world, even the Body and Blood of my dearest Savior.

O take from me all affection to sin and vanity; let not my affections dwell below, but soar upwards to the element of love, to the seat of God, the regions of glory, and the inheritance of Jesus; that I may hunger and thirst for the bread of life, and the wine of elect souls, and may know no loves but the love of God, and the most merciful Jesus. Amen.

— *Jeremy Taylor*

234　LORD Jesus Christ, Son of the living God, we pray you to set your passion, cross, and death between your judgment and our souls, now and in the hour of our death. Give mercy and grace to the living; pardon and rest to the dead; to your holy Church peace and concord; and to us sinners everlasting life and glory; for with the Father and Holy Spirit you live and reign, one God, now and for ever. Amen.

— From the *Office of the Hours*

Index of Subjects

[Numbers refer to the entries, not to the pages]

Notes on Authors

ALEXANDER, CECIL FRANCES, 1823-1895; author of many hymns, especially famous for those for children; wife of Archbishop William Alexander of Armagh, Ireland.

ALFORD, HENRY, 1810-1871; scholar, poet, musician, artist; Dean of Canterbury, 1857-1871.

ASTLEY, SIR JACOB, 1579-1652; prayer at battle of Edgehill, 1642, by King Charles I's general of foot soldiers in the First Civil War.

AUGUSTINE, SAINT, 354-430; most influential theologian of the Western Church; Bishop of Hippo Regius in North Africa (modern Bona in Algeria), 396-430.

BARCLAY, WILLIAM, 1907-1978; minister of the Church of Scotland; Lecturer in New Testament, 1946-1963, and Professor of Divinity, 1963-1974, in the University of Glasgow.

BELL, MAURICE FREDERICK, 1862-1931; priest of the Church of England; author of *Church Music*, 1922; contributor to *The English Hymnal*, 1906.

BENSON, WILLIAM MEUX, 1824-1915; a founder of the Society of Saint John the Evangelist, known as the Cowley Fathers.

BIANCO DA SIENA, *ca.* 1367-1434; member of the Order of Jesuates; the hymn is from his *Laudi spirituali*.

BLACK, HUGH, 1868-1953; minister of the Free Church of Scotland; Professor of Practical Theology, Union Theological Seminary, New York City, 1906-1938.

BONAR, HORATIUS, 1808-1889; minister of the Free Church of Scotland and its Moderator in 1883.

BOWIE, WALTER RUSSELL, 1882-1969; Rector of St. Paul's, Richmond, Va., 1911-1923, and Grace Church, New York City, 1923-1939; Professor at Union Theological Seminary, 1939-1950, and Virginia Theological Seminary, 1950-1955.

BRENT, CHARLES HENRY, 1862-1929; Bishop of the Philippines, 1901-1918, and of Western New York, 1918-1929; a founder of the modern Ecumenical Movement.

BRIGHT, WILLIAM, 1824-1901; Regius Professor of Ecclesiastical History and Canon of Christ Church, Oxford, 1868-1901.

BURROUGHS, EDWARD ARTHUR, 1882-1935; Canon of Peterborough, 1917-1922; Dean of Bristol, 1922-1926; Bishop of Ripon, 1926-1935.

CRANMER, THOMAS, 1489-1556; Archbishop of Canterbury, 1533-1556; principal compiler of the Book of Common Prayer.

DEARMER, PERCY, 1867-1936; Professor of Ecclesiastical Art, King's College, London, 1919-1932; Canon of Westminster, 1931-1936.

DONNE, JOHN, 1573-1631; eminent poet and preacher; Dean of St. Paul's Cathedral, London, 1622-1631.

DOWDEN, JOHN, 1840-1910; liturgical scholar of the Episcopal Church of Scotland; Bishop of Edinburgh, 1886-1910.

ELLERTON, JOHN, 1826-1893; priest of the Church of England; author and editor of many hymn books.

FORTUNATUS, VENANTIUS HONORIUS, *ca.* 540-600; chaplain of the convent of the Holy Cross, Poitiers, and Bishop of Poitiers, 599.

FRANCIS OF ASSISI, SAINT, 1182-1226; founder of the Order of Friars Minor, known as the Franciscans.

HERRICK, ROBERT, 1591-1674; poet, and priest of the Church of England; Vicar of Dean Prior, Devonshire, 1629-1648, 1662-1674.

HUNTER, JOHN, 1848-1917; Congregationalist minister of Trinity, Glasgow, 1881-1901, 1904-1911, and of King's Weigh House Congregational Church, London, 1901-1904.

JAMES, LIONEL, 1868-1948; classical scholar; Headmaster of Monmouth Grammar School, 1906-1927.

KEN, THOMAS, 1637-1711; a royal chaplain to King Charles II; Bishop of Bath and Wells, 1685-1691; deprived for refusal to take the oath to William and Mary.

LAUD, WILLIAM, 1573-1645; President and benefactor of St. John's College, Oxford, 1611-1621, and Chancellor of the University from 1630; Bishop of St. David's, Wales, 1621-1626, of Bath and Wells, 1626-1628, of London, 1628-1633, and Archbishop of Canterbury, 1633-1645.

LITTLEDALE, RICHARD FREDERICK, 1833-1890; priest of the Church of England; liturgical scholar and hymnodist.

LOYOLA, IGNATIUS, SAINT, 1491-1556; founder in 1540 of the Society of Jesus, known as the Jesuits.

MARTIN, HUGH, 1890-1964; Baptist minister; Assistant Secretary of the Student Christian Movement, 1914-1929, and manager and editor of its Press, 1929-1950; Moderator of the National Free Church Federal Council, 1952-1953; Vice-President of the British Council of Churches, 1950-1952, and chairman of its Executive Committee, 1956-1962.

MARTINEAU, JAMES, 1805-1900; Unitarian minister; Professor of Mental and Moral Philosophy, New Manchester College, and its Principal from 1869.

MASEFIELD, JOHN, 1878-1967; English poet, dramatist, and novelist; appointed Poet Laureate in 1930.

MILLER, SAMUEL HOWARD, 1900-1968; minister of Old Cambridge Baptist Church, 1935-1959; Professor of Pastoral Theology, 1958-1959, and Dean, 1959-1968, of the Divinity School of Harvard University.

MILNER-WHITE, ERIC, 1884-1963; Chaplain, 1912-1941, and Dean, 1918-1941, of King's College, Cambridge; Dean of York, 1941-1963.

MILTON, JOHN, 1608-1674; eminent poet and writer in English and Latin; secretary to Oliver Cromwell; Puritan controversialist of independent opinions; the "Ode on the Morning of Christ's Nativity" was composed in 1629.

NASH, HENRY SYLVESTER, 1854-1912; Professor of New Testament, Episcopal Theological School, Cambridge, Mass., 1882-1912.

NEALE, JOHN MASON, 1818-1866; scholar of church history and liturgy; hymnodist and translator of Greek and Latin hymns; founder of Sisterhood of St. Margaret, 1856; Warden of Sackville College, East Grinstead.

NIEBUHR, REINHOLD, 1892-1971; influential American theologian; minister of the Evangelical Synod of North America; Professor of Philosophy of Religion, 1928-1930, and of Ethics, 1930-1960, Union Theological Seminary, New York City.

OOSTERHUIS, HUUB, 1933-; Dutch theologian and liturgist; priest of the Society of Jesus, 1964-1969; chaplain at the University of Amsterdam.

ORCHARD, WILLIAM EDWIN, 1877-1955; liturgist and ecumenist; ordained a Presbyterian minister in 1904, he began a notable ministry at King's Weigh House Congregational Church, London, in 1914; became a Roman Catholic in 1932, and made priest, 1935.

PAGET, FRANCIS, 1851-1911; Regius Professor of Pastoral Theology and Canon of Christ Church, Oxford, 1885-1892, and Dean, 1892-1901; Bishop of Oxford, 1901-1911.

PARSONS, EDWARD LAMBE, 1868-1960; Rector of St. Mark's, Berkeley, 1904-1919; Bishop Coadjutor, 1919-1924, and Bishop of California, 1924-1940.

PATRICK, SAINT, *ca.* 385-461; missionary Bishop of Ireland, 432-461; patron saint of the Irish people.

PRICE, CHARLES PHILIP, 1920-; Preacher to Harvard University, 1963-1972; Professor of Systematic Theology, Virginia Theological Seminary, Alexandria, Va., 1956-1963, 1972-.

REYNOLDS, EDWARD, 1599-1676; Vicar of St. Lawrence, Jewry, London, 1645-1662; Dean of Christ Church, Oxford, 1648-1650, 1659; Bishop of Norwich, 1661-1676.

RICHARD OF WYCHE, SAINT, *ca.* 1197-1253; scholar, pastor; Chancellor of Archbishop Edmund Rich of Canterbury; Bishop of Chichester, 1245-1253.

ROBBINS, HOWARD CHANDLER, 1876-1952; Dean of the Cathedral of St. John the Divine, 1917-1929, and Professor of Pastoral Theology, General Theological Seminary, 1929-1944, New York City.

ROSSETTI, CHRISTINA GEORGINA, 1830-1894; English lyric poet; composer of devotional manuals.

SHEPHERD, MASSEY HAMILTON, JR., 1913-; Professor of Church History, Episcopal Theological School, Cambridge, Mass., 1940-1954; Hodges Professor of Liturgics, The Church Divinity School of the Pacific, Berkeley, Calif., since 1954.

SUTER, JOHN WALLACE, JR., 1890-1977; Rector of Church of the Epiphany, New York City, 1933-1944; Dean of Washington Cathedral, 1944-1950; Custodian of the Standard Book of Common Prayer, 1942-1963.

TAYLOR, JEREMY, 1613-1667; theologian, moralist, and devotional writer; parish priest of the Church of England, and chaplain to Archbishop William Laud and King Charles I; Bishop of Down and Connor, Ireland, 1661-1667.

TEMPLE, WILLIAM, 1881-1944; theologian and philosopher; Bishop of Manchester, 1921-1929; Archbishop of York, 1929-1942; Archbishop of Canterbury, 1942-1944; ecumenical leader.

THOMAS A KEMPIS, *ca.* 1380-1471; member of the Brethren of the Common Life in Zwolle, Holland from 1399, and sub-prior from 1425; his *Imitation of Christ* has been translated into more languages than any other book, except the Bible.

TRENHOLME, EDWARD CRAIG, S.S.J.E., d. 1949; early ministry in Ontario, Canada; priest and member of the Society of St. John the Evangelist in Boston, London, and Oxford.

VAUGHAN, CHARLES JOHN, 1816-1897; Headmaster of Harrow, 1844-1859; Master of the Temple, 1869-1894; Dean of Llandaff, 1879-1896; a founder and president (1894) of the University College of Cardiff.

WESLEY, CHARLES, 1707-1788; priest of the Church of England; a founder, with this brother John, of the Methodist Movement; itinerant preacher; author of some 6,500 hymns.

WESLEY, JOHN, 1703-1791; priest of the Church of England; the founder of the Methodist Movement; itinerant preacher, scholar, author and translator of hymns.

WILLIAMS, ROWLAND, 1817-1870; Vice-Principal and Professor of Hebrew, St. David's Theological College, Lampeter, Wales, 1850-1863; Vicar of Briad Chalke, 1858-1870.

XAVIER, FRANCIS, SAINT, 1506-1552; a founder of the Society of Jesus; Jesuit missionary in the Portuguese empire in India, Malacca, and the Moluccas; first Christian missionary to Japan.

Acknowledgments

The following publishers and persons have graciously given permission to use copyrighted material in this book. The numbers refer to the formularies in this collection.

For published materials of my own:

AUGSBURG PUBLISHING HOUSE — for 21, 30 (first four lines), 37, from *A Liturgical Psalter for the Christian Year,* © 1976 by Massey H. Shepherd, Jr.

THE CONSULTATION ON CHURCH UNION — for 222, from *An Order of Worship,* © 1968 by the Executive Committee of the Consultation on Church Union; Published by Forward Movement Publications.

THE DIOCESE OF BETHLEHEM — for 24, 114.

For materials from liturgical books and hymnals:

THE REVEREND CANON CHARLES MORTIMER GUILBERT, as Custodian of the *Standard Book of Common Prayer* — for 6, 27, 111, 209, 214, from *Services for Trial Use,* © 1971; for 143, from *Prayers, Thanksgivings, Litanies,* © 1973; and for 18, 32, from *The Book of Common Prayer (Proposed)* © 1977.

CENTRAL BOARD OF FINANCE OF THE CHURCH OF ENGLAND — for 63, 138, 204, from *The Prayer Book as Proposed in 1928,* with the permission of the holders of the copyright.

THE PUBLICATION COMMITTEE OF THE EPISCOPAL CHURCH OF SCOTLAND — for 135, from the Scottish *Book of Common Prayer*, 1929.

THE FAITH PRESS LTD. — for 215, from *The Eucharistic Liturgy of Taizé*, © 1962 by the Taizé Community.

A. R. MOWBRAY AND CO. LTD. — for 39, 136, 150, from *After the Third Collect*, edited by E. Milner-White, Third Edition, 1952.

OXFORD UNIVERSITY PRESS, LONDON — for 115, 173, from *The Cuddesdon College Office Book*, New Edition, 1961; and for 212, 217, from *The Order of Divine Service for Public Worship* [Compiled by W. E. Orchard], 1919. And from its Music Department for 175 (four stanzas) from *The English Hymnal*, 1906.

OXFORD UNIVERSITY PRESS, New York — for 82, 100, from *The Kingdom, the Power, and the Glory*, An American Edition of the Grey Book, © 1933; renewed 1961 by Bradford Young.

THE PAULIST PRESS — for 154, 170, 187, from Huub Oosterhuis, *Your Word is Near*, © 1968 by The Missionary Society of St. Paul the Apostle in the State of New York.

STUDENT CHRISTIAN MOVEMENT PRESS LTD., and WM. B. EERDMANS PUBLISHING CO. — for 118, 169, 171, 191, from *Contemporary Prayers for Public Worship*, edited by Caryl Micklem, © 1967 by SCM Press Ltd.

THE WESTMINSTER PRESS — for 155, from *The Book of Common Worship*, © 1946 by the Board of Christian Education of the Presbyterian Church in the United States of America.

For materials from anthologies
for both public and personal use:

ABINGDON PRESS — for 105, 203, 216, from Walter Russell Bowie, *Lift Up Your Hearts*, © renewal 1967 by Walter Russell Bowie.

ASSOCIATED PARISHES, INC. — for 221, from *In Newness of Life*.

THE BRITISH BROADCASTING CORPORATION — for 68, 78, 90, 92, 121, 122, 125, 166, from *New Every Morning*, Revised Edition, 1961.

THE REVEREND F. D. G. CAMPBELL, S.S.J.E., Superior General of the Society of Saint John the Evangelist — for 219.

WILLIAM COLLINS SONS AND CO. LTD. — for 66, from William Barclay, *The Plain Man's Book of Prayers*, © 1959 by William Barclay.

FORWARD MOVEMENT PUBLICATIONS, 412 Sycamore Street, Cincinnati, Ohio 45202 — for 62, 67, 76, from *Prayers for all Occasions*, Eleventh Edition.

HARPER AND ROW PUBLISHERS, INC. — for 108, from *Adventures in Prayer*, selected by Charles Henry Brent, edited by S.S. Drury. Copyright © 1932 by Harper and Row Publishers; and for 5, 43, 56, 72, 119, 172, 186, 225, 232 from *Prayers for Daily Use*. Copyright © 1957 by Samuel H. Miller.

HODDER AND STOUGHTON LTD. — for 84, 88, 107, from *Parish Prayers*, Compiled and Edited by Frank Colquhoun, 1967.

A. R. MOWBRAY AND CO., LTD. — for 100, 123, 167, from *The Prayer Manual*, Compiled by Frederick B. MacNutt, Fourth Edition, 1968.

THE SOCIETY FOR PROMOTING CHRISTIAN KNOWLEDGE — for 124, from *Acts of Devotion*, 1928; for 173, 179, 201, 224, from *My God My Glory*, 1967; and for 184, from *A Procession of Passion Prayers*, 1956, both of the latter two by Eric Milner-White.

STUDENT CHRISTIAN MOVEMENT PRESS LTD. — for 139, from *Prayers of Health and Healing*, 1932; for 65, 71, 75, 79, 101, from *A Book of Prayers for Schools*, edited by Hugh Martin, 1936; for 106, 140-142, from *Prayers in Time of War*, edited by Hugh Martin, 1939-1940.

For poetry:

MACMILLAN PUBLISHING CO., INC. — for 163, excerpts from John Masefield, *The Coming of Christ*, © 1928 by John Masefield, renewed 1956 by John Masefield; and for 190, from John Masefield, *Easter, A Play for Singers*, © 1929 by Macmillan Publishing Co., Inc., renewed 1957 by John Masefield.